KING ARTHUR

EXCALIBUR UNSHEATHED

AN ENGLISH LEGEND

GRAPHIC UNIVERSE™

STORY BY
JEFF LIMKE

PENCILS AND INKS BY
THOMAS YEATES

ADAPTED FROM
SIR THOMAS MALORY'S
LE MORTE D'ARTHUR

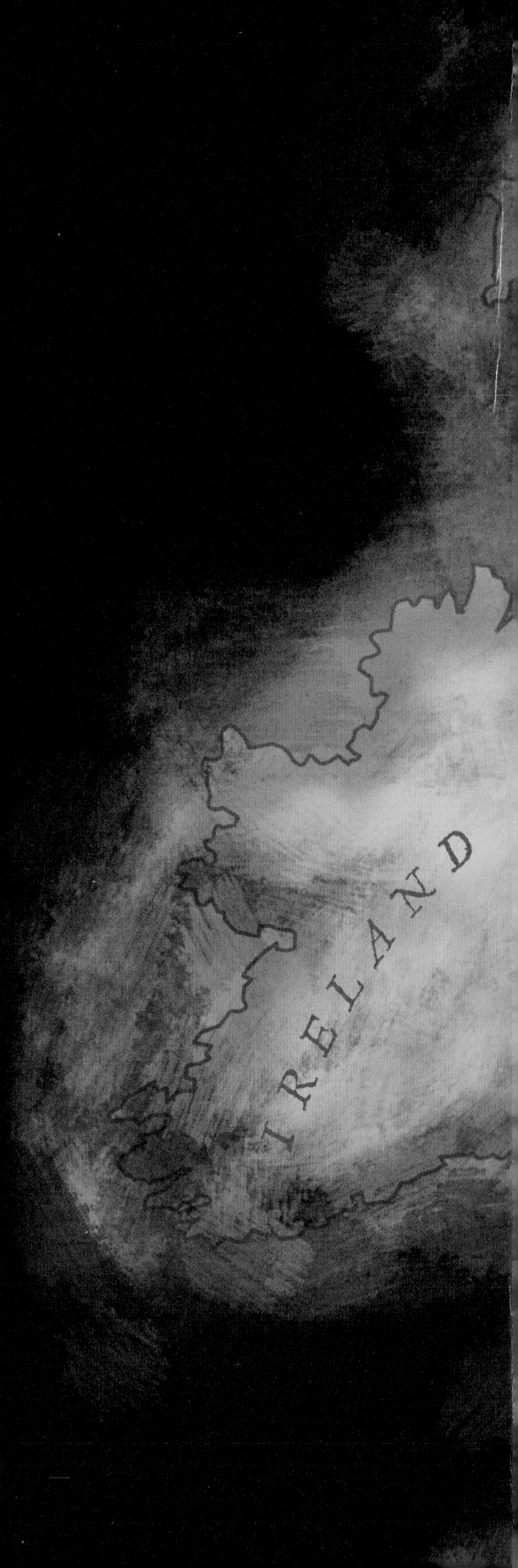
IRELAND

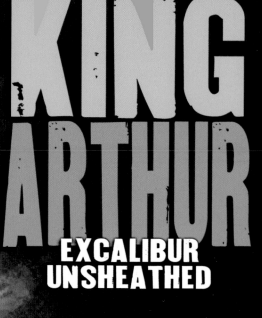

KING ARTHUR

EXCALIBUR UNSHEATHED

AN ENGLISH LEGEND

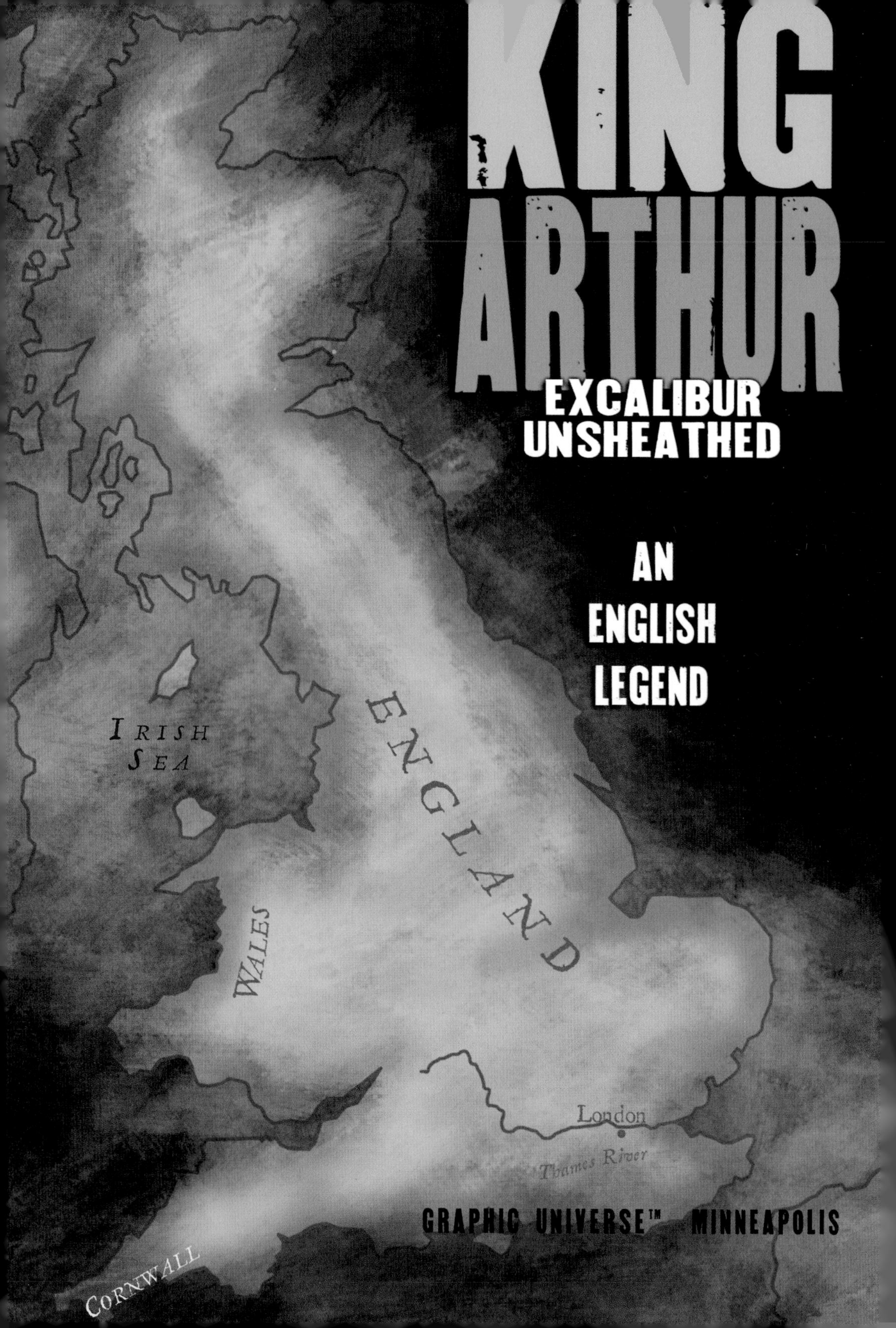

IRISH SEA

ENGLAND

WALES

London
Thames River

CORNWALL

GRAPHIC UNIVERSE™ · MINNEAPOLIS

Whether King Arthur was a real person is unknown, but his story is set amid real events in British history. He would have lived around A.D. 400 or 500, when the many small kingdoms of England, Wales, and Cornwall were fighting each other and against foreign invaders. Arthur is thus seen as the king who united and defended early Britain. But often Arthurian tales are depicted as taking place much later in the Middle Ages (about 1100–1300), with knights in armor, jousts, and castles. **Excalibur Unsheathed** follows that tradition.

STORY BY JEFF LIMKE

PENCILS AND INKS BY THOMAS YEATES
SPECIAL THANKS TO TOD SMITH

COLORING BY HI-FI DESIGN

LETTERING BY BILL HAUSER

Graphic Universe
A division of Lerner Publishing Group, Inc.
241 First Avenue North
Minneapolis, MN 55401 USA

For reading levels and more information, look up this title at www.lernerbooks.com.

Library of Congress Cataloging-in-Publication Data

Limke, Jeff.
    King Arthur : Excalibur unsheathed / by Jeff Limke, adapted from Sir Thomas Malory's Le Morte d'Arthur ; illustrations by Thomas Yeates.
        p.   cm. — (Graphic myths and legends)
    Includes index.
    ISBN 978-0-8225-3083-1 (lib. bdg. : alk. paper)
    ISBN 978-0-8225-7217-6 (EB pdf)
    1. Graphic novels. I. Malory, Thomas, Sir, 15th cent. Morte d'Arthur. II. Title. III. Series.
PN6727.L53S76 2007
741.5'973—dc22   2005010186

Manufactured in the United States of America
7-52813-3788-2/25/2022

TABLE OF CONTENTS

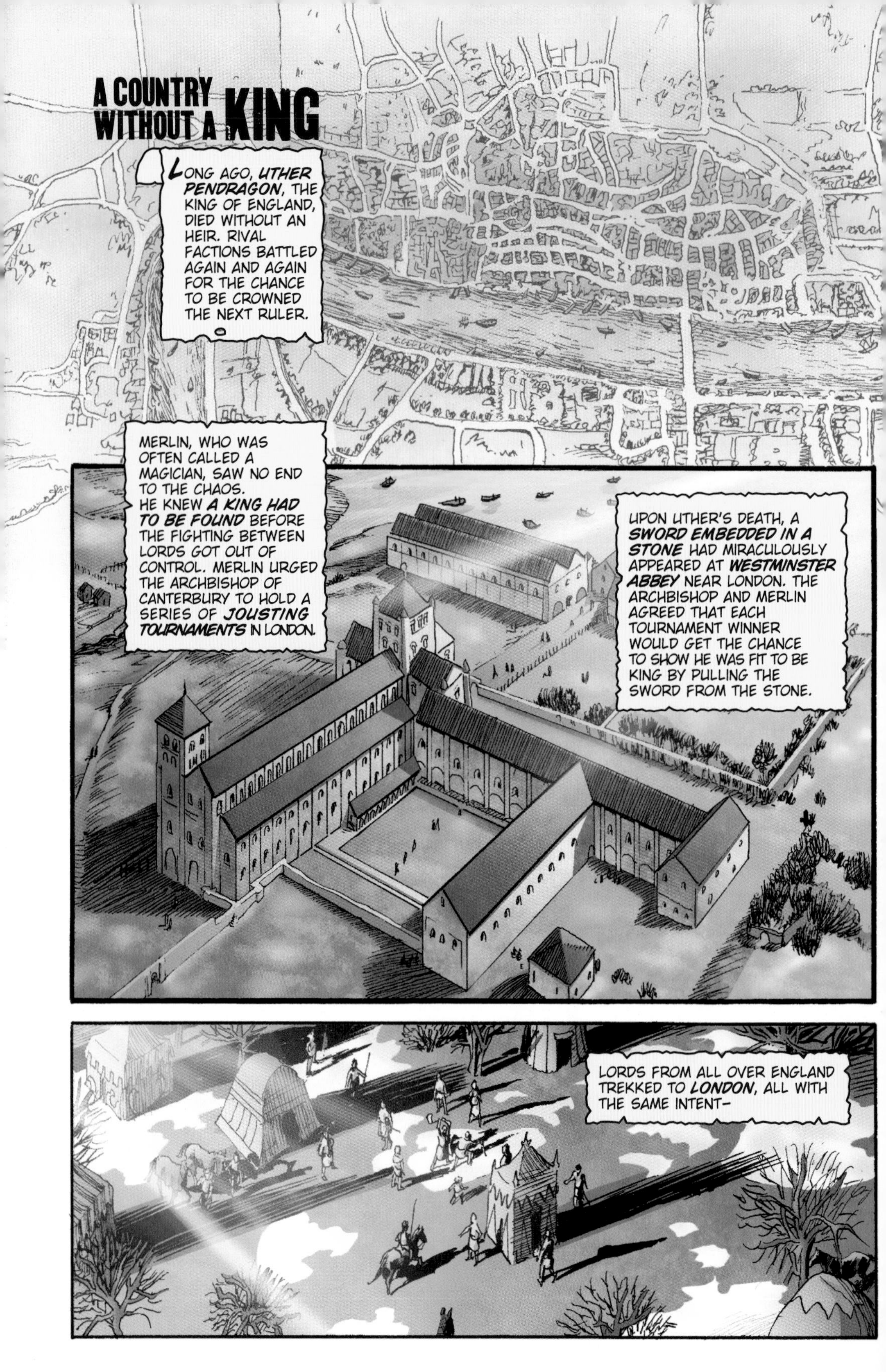
A COUNTRY WITHOUT A KING
LONG AGO, UTHER PENDRAGON, THE KING OF ENGLAND, DIED WITHOUT AN HEIR. RIVAL FACTIONS BATTLED AGAIN AND AGAIN FOR THE CHANCE TO BE CROWNED THE NEXT RULER.
MERLIN, WHO WAS OFTEN CALLED A MAGICIAN, SAW NO END TO THE CHAOS. HE KNEW A KING HAD TO BE FOUND BEFORE THE FIGHTING BETWEEN LORDS GOT OUT OF CONTROL. MERLIN URGED THE ARCHBISHOP OF CANTERBURY TO HOLD A SERIES OF JOUSTING TOURNAMENTS IN LONDON.
UPON UTHER'S DEATH, A SWORD EMBEDDED IN A STONE HAD MIRACULOUSLY APPEARED AT WESTMINSTER ABBEY NEAR LONDON. THE ARCHBISHOP AND MERLIN AGREED THAT EACH TOURNAMENT WINNER WOULD GET THE CHANCE TO SHOW HE WAS FIT TO BE KING BY PULLING THE SWORD FROM THE STONE.
LORDS FROM ALL OVER ENGLAND TREKKED TO LONDON, ALL WITH THE SAME INTENT-

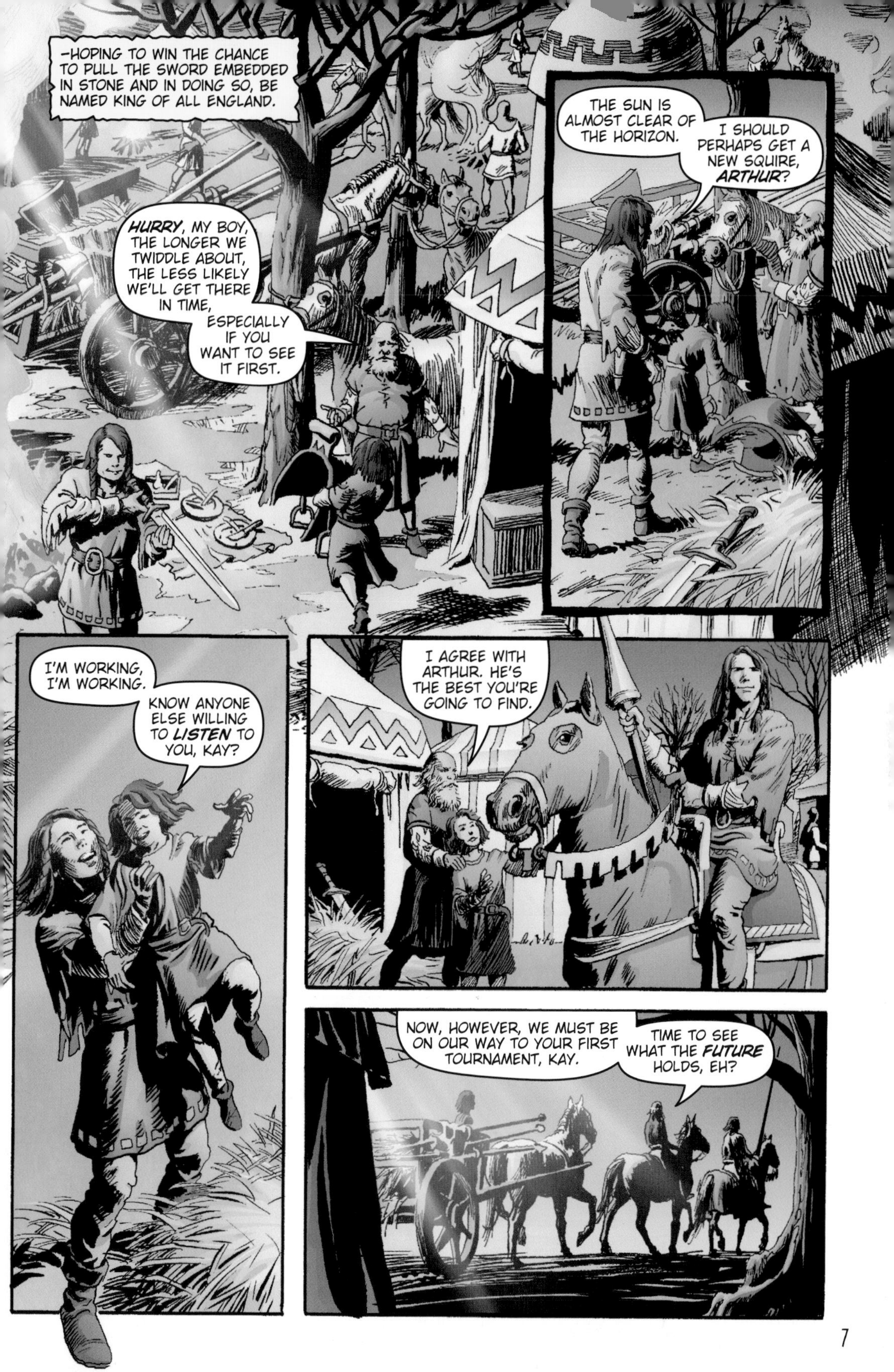

–HOPING TO WIN THE CHANCE TO PULL THE SWORD EMBEDDED IN STONE AND IN DOING SO, BE NAMED KING OF ALL ENGLAND.
HURRY, MY BOY, THE LONGER WE TWIDDLE ABOUT, THE LESS LIKELY WE'LL GET THERE IN TIME,
ESPECIALLY IF YOU WANT TO SEE IT FIRST.
THE SUN IS ALMOST CLEAR OF THE HORIZON.
I SHOULD PERHAPS GET A NEW SQUIRE, ARTHUR?
I'M WORKING, I'M WORKING.
KNOW ANYONE ELSE WILLING TO LISTEN TO YOU, KAY?
I AGREE WITH ARTHUR. HE'S THE BEST YOU'RE GOING TO FIND.
NOW, HOWEVER, WE MUST BE ON OUR WAY TO YOUR FIRST TOURNAMENT, KAY.
TIME TO SEE WHAT THE FUTURE HOLDS, EH?

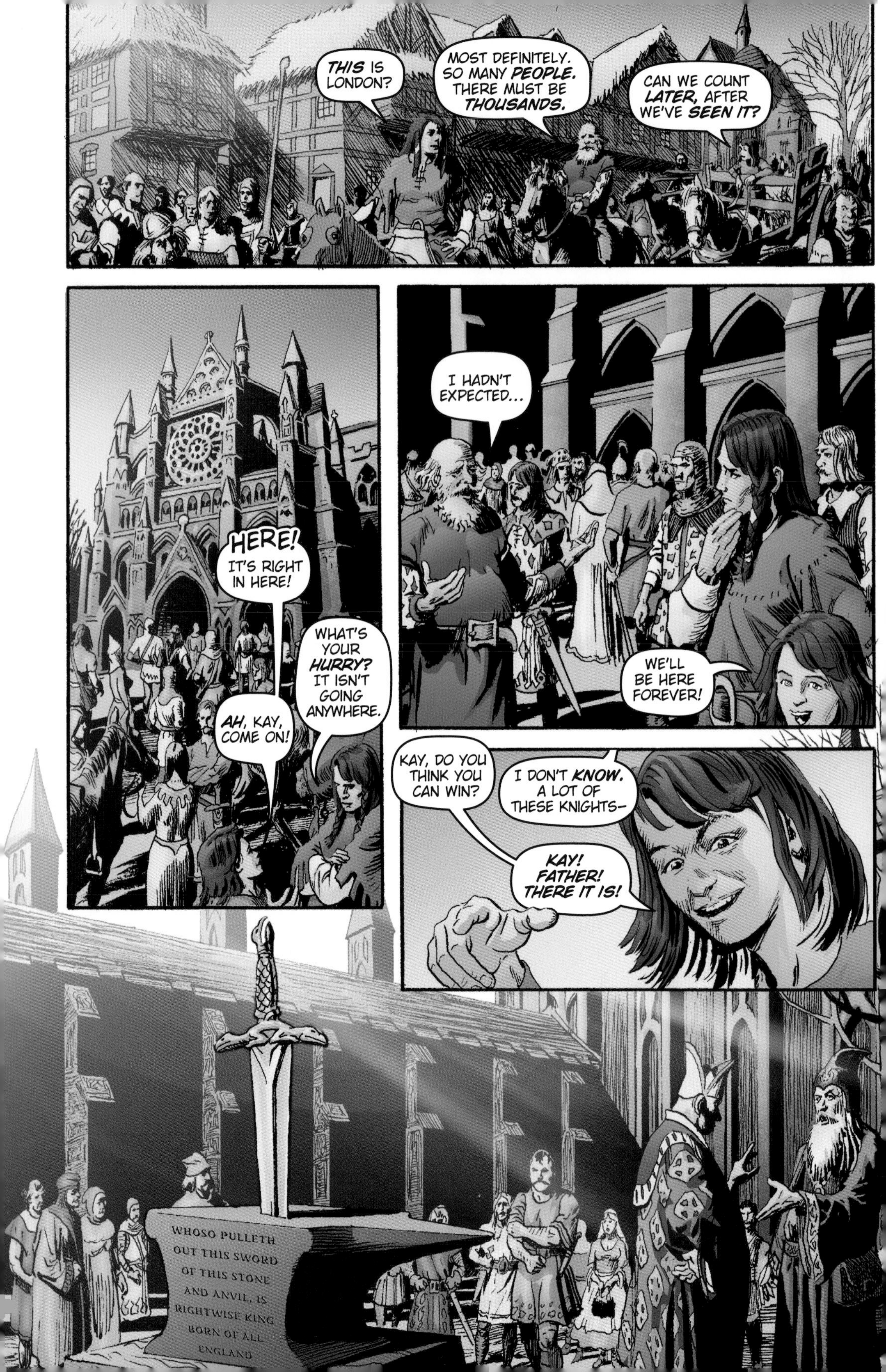
THIS IS LONDON?
MOST DEFINITELY. SO MANY PEOPLE. THERE MUST BE THOUSANDS.
CAN WE COUNT LATER, AFTER WE'VE SEEN IT?
HERE! IT'S RIGHT IN HERE!
WHAT'S YOUR HURRY? IT ISN'T GOING ANYWHERE.
AH, KAY, COME ON!
I HADN'T EXPECTED...
WE'LL BE HERE FOREVER!
KAY, DO YOU THINK YOU CAN WIN?
I DON'T KNOW. A LOT OF THESE KNIGHTS–
KAY! FATHER! THERE IT IS!
WHOSO PULLETH OUT THIS SWORD OF THIS STONE AND ANVIL, IS RIGHTWISE KING BORN OF ALL ENGLAND

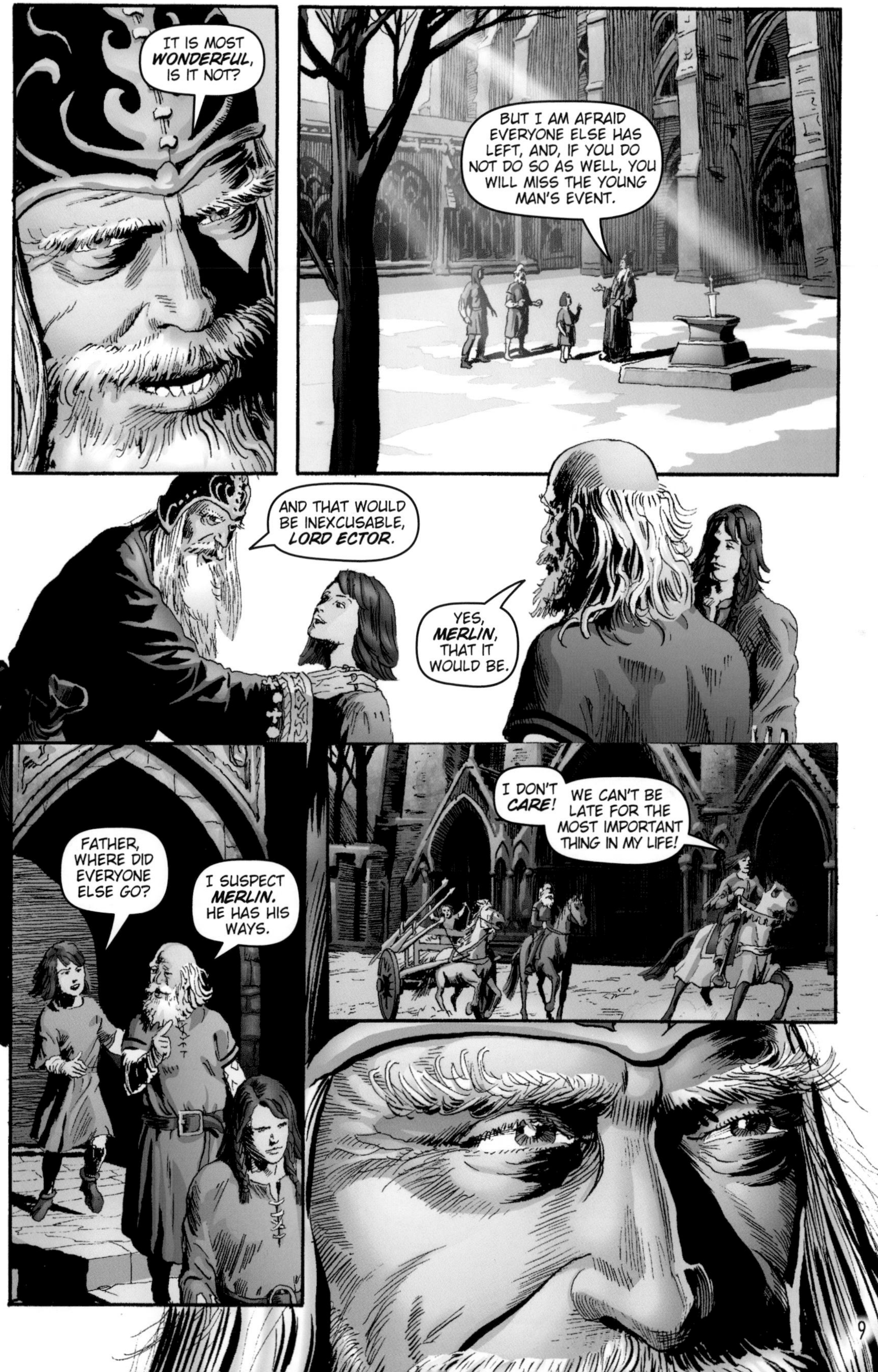
IT IS MOST WONDERFUL, IS IT NOT?
BUT I AM AFRAID EVERYONE ELSE HAS LEFT, AND, IF YOU DO NOT DO SO AS WELL, YOU WILL MISS THE YOUNG MAN'S EVENT.
AND THAT WOULD BE INEXCUSABLE, LORD ECTOR.
YES, MERLIN, THAT IT WOULD BE.
FATHER, WHERE DID EVERYONE ELSE GO?
I SUSPECT MERLIN. HE HAS HIS WAYS.
I DON'T CARE!
WE CAN'T BE LATE FOR THE MOST IMPORTANT THING IN MY LIFE!

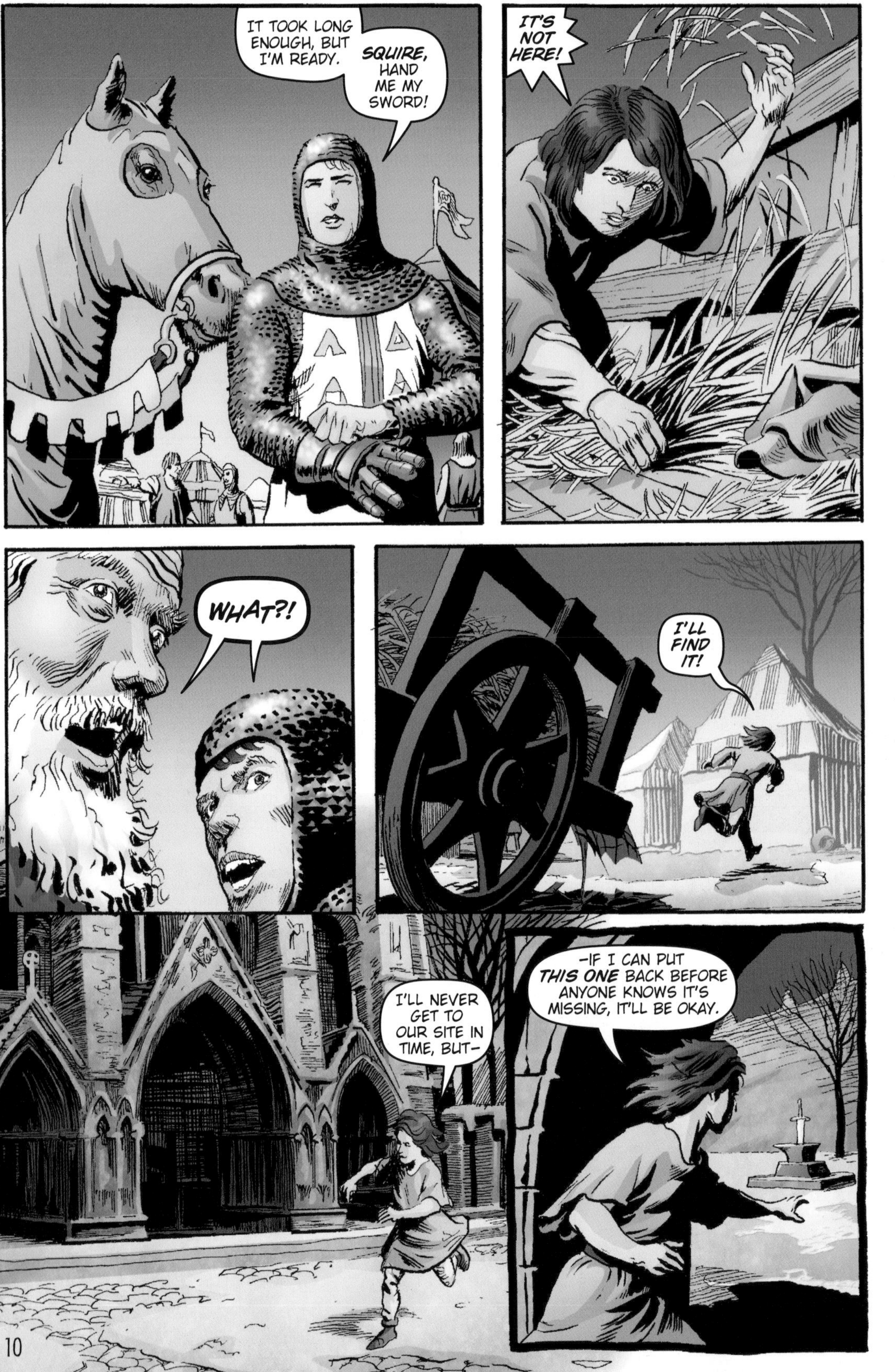
IT TOOK LONG ENOUGH, BUT I'M READY.
SQUIRE, HAND ME MY SWORD!
IT'S NOT HERE!
WHAT?!
I'LL FIND IT!
I'LL NEVER GET TO OUR SITE IN TIME, BUT–
–IF I CAN PUT THIS ONE BACK BEFORE ANYONE KNOWS IT'S MISSING, IT'LL BE OKAY.

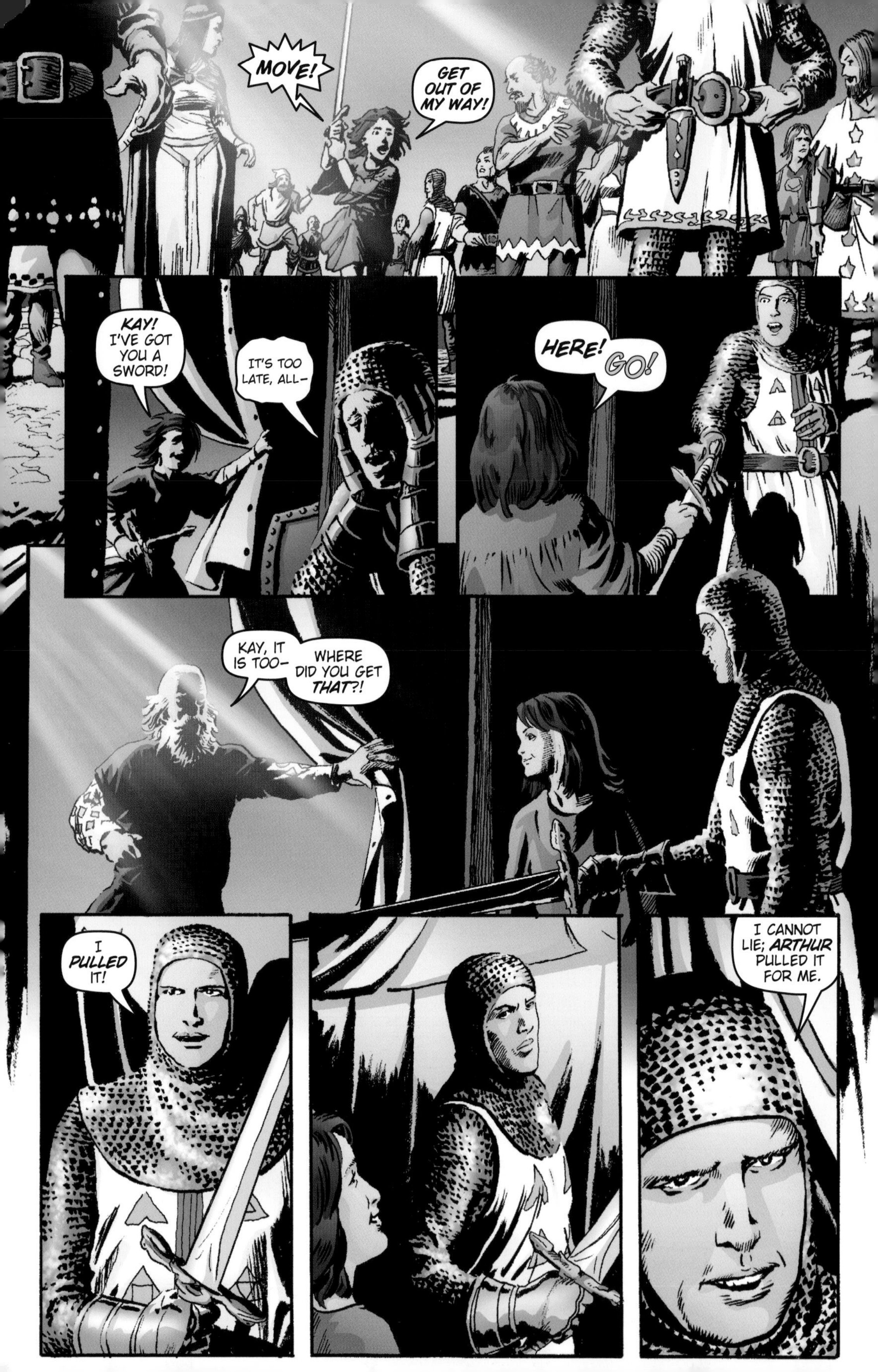
MOVE!
GET OUT OF MY WAY!
KAY! I'VE GOT YOU A SWORD!
IT'S TOO LATE, ALL-
HERE! GO!
KAY, IT IS TOO-
WHERE DID YOU GET THAT?!
I PULLED IT!
I CANNOT LIE; ARTHUR PULLED IT FOR ME.

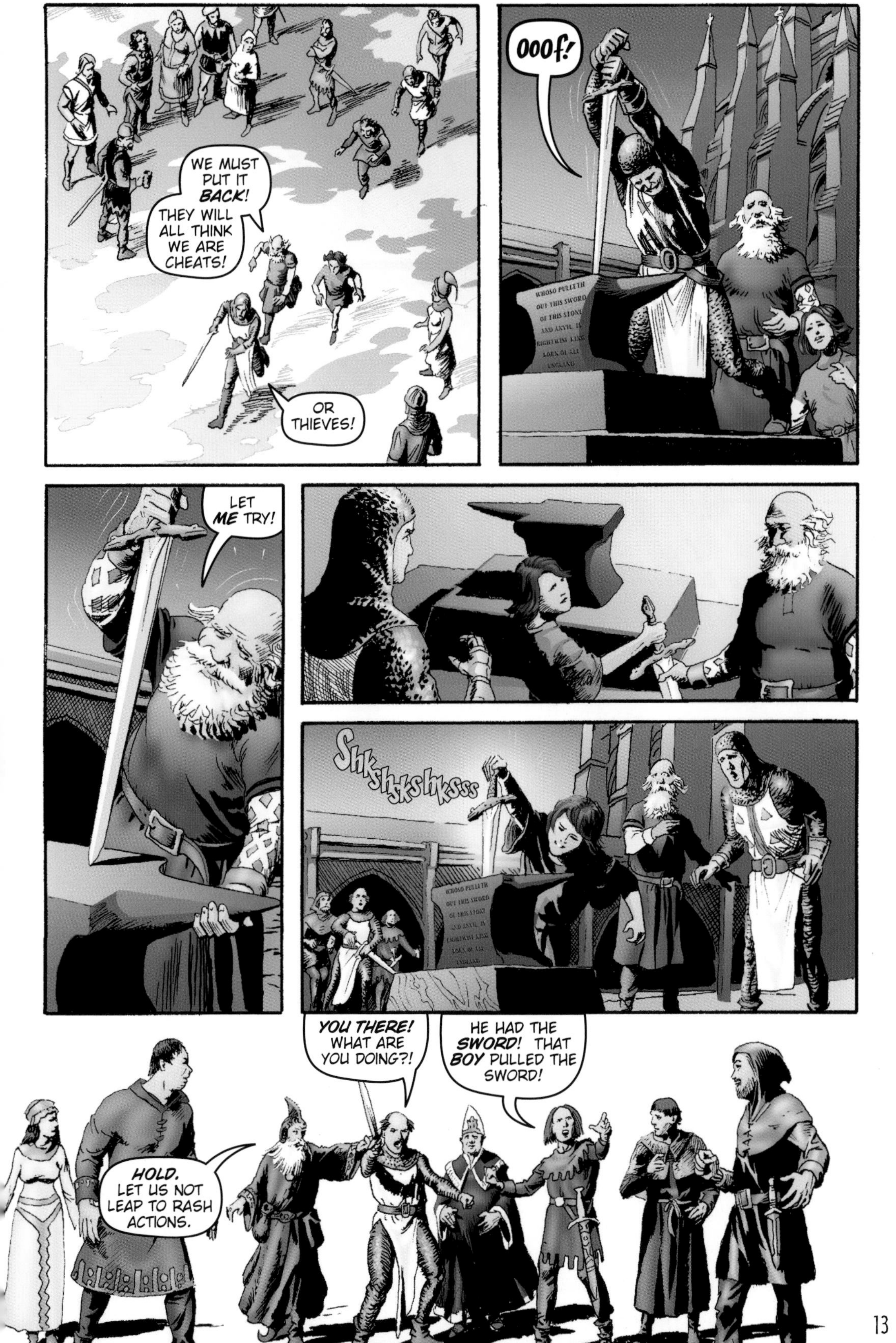

WE MUST PUT IT *BACK*! THEY WILL ALL THINK WE ARE CHEATS!
OR THIEVES!
OOOF!
WHOSO PULLETH OUT THIS SWORD
LET *ME* TRY!
SHKSHKSHKSSS
YOU THERE! WHAT ARE YOU DOING?!
HE HAD THE *SWORD!* THAT *BOY* PULLED THE SWORD!
HOLD. LET US NOT LEAP TO RASH ACTIONS.

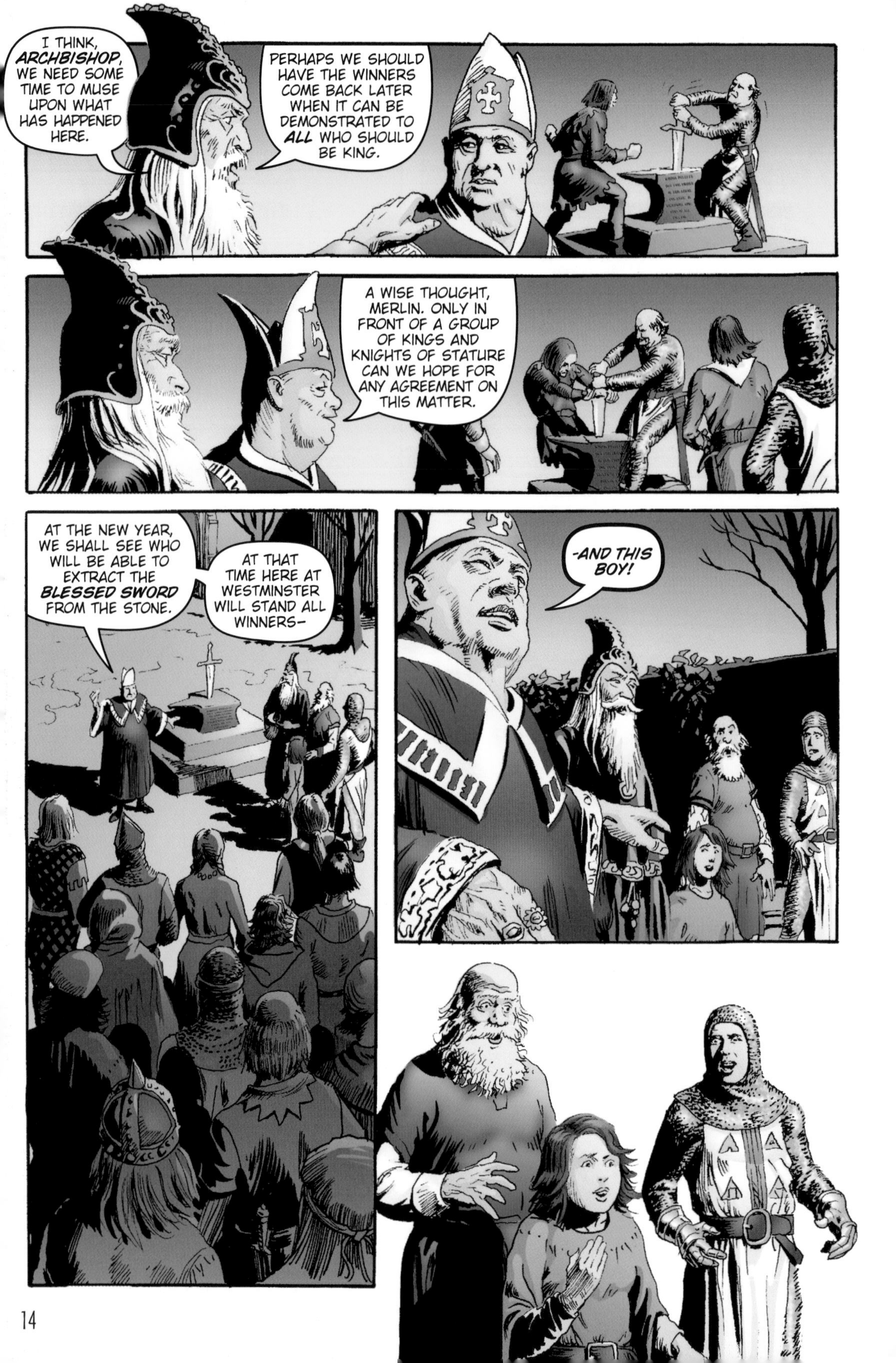
I THINK, ARCHBISHOP, WE NEED SOME TIME TO MUSE UPON WHAT HAS HAPPENED HERE.
PERHAPS WE SHOULD HAVE THE WINNERS COME BACK LATER WHEN IT CAN BE DEMONSTRATED TO ALL WHO SHOULD BE KING.
A WISE THOUGHT, MERLIN. ONLY IN FRONT OF A GROUP OF KINGS AND KNIGHTS OF STATURE CAN WE HOPE FOR ANY AGREEMENT ON THIS MATTER.
AT THE NEW YEAR, WE SHALL SEE WHO WILL BE ABLE TO EXTRACT THE BLESSED SWORD FROM THE STONE.
AT THAT TIME HERE AT WESTMINSTER WILL STAND ALL WINNERS–
–AND THIS BOY!

THE NEW KING IN A NEW YEAR

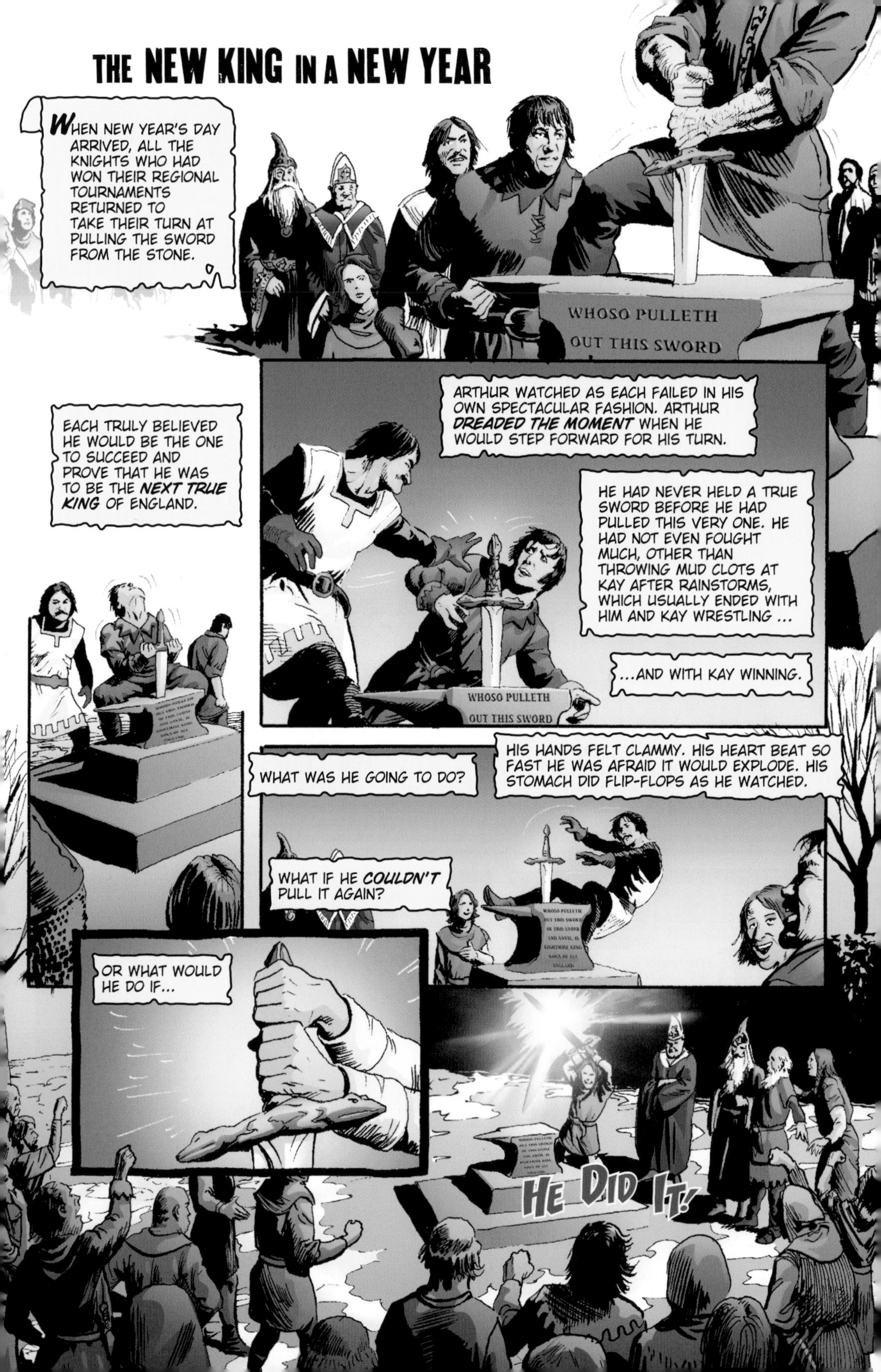
WHEN NEW YEAR'S DAY ARRIVED, ALL THE KNIGHTS WHO HAD WON THEIR REGIONAL TOURNAMENTS RETURNED TO TAKE THEIR TURN AT PULLING THE SWORD FROM THE STONE.
WHOSO PULLETH OUT THIS SWORD
EACH TRULY BELIEVED HE WOULD BE THE ONE TO SUCCEED AND PROVE THAT HE WAS TO BE THE ***NEXT TRUE KING*** OF ENGLAND.
ARTHUR WATCHED AS EACH FAILED IN HIS OWN SPECTACULAR FASHION. ARTHUR ***DREADED THE MOMENT*** WHEN HE WOULD STEP FORWARD FOR HIS TURN.
HE HAD NEVER HELD A TRUE SWORD BEFORE HE HAD PULLED THIS VERY ONE. HE HAD NOT EVEN FOUGHT MUCH, OTHER THAN THROWING MUD CLOTS AT KAY AFTER RAINSTORMS, WHICH USUALLY ENDED WITH HIM AND KAY WRESTLING ...
...AND WITH KAY WINNING.
WHOSO PULLETH OUT THIS SWORD
WHAT WAS HE GOING TO DO?
HIS HANDS FELT CLAMMY. HIS HEART BEAT SO FAST HE WAS AFRAID IT WOULD EXPLODE. HIS STOMACH DID FLIP-FLOPS AS HE WATCHED.
WHAT IF HE ***COULDN'T*** PULL IT AGAIN?
OR WHAT WOULD HE DO IF...
HE DID IT!

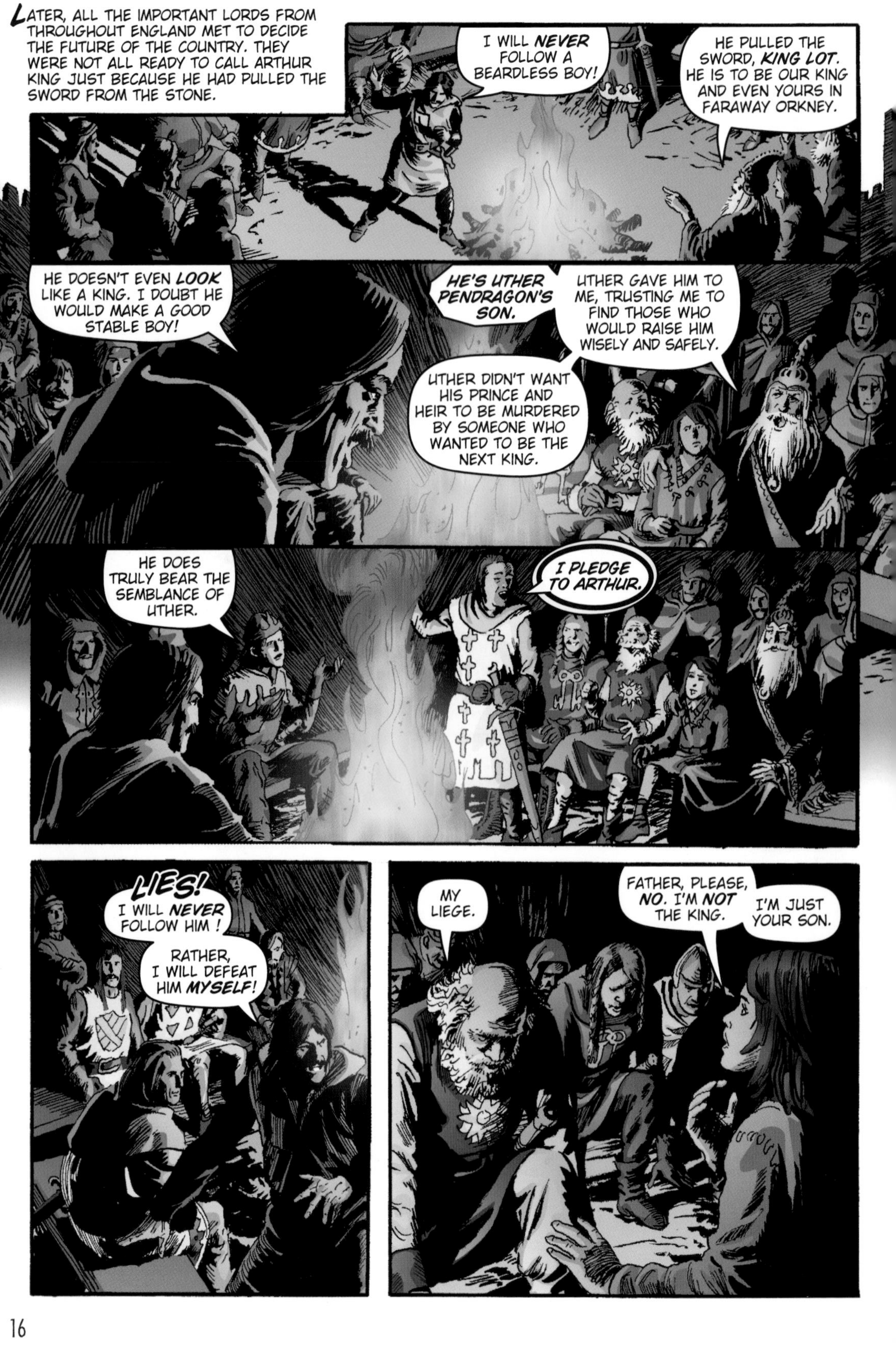
LATER, ALL THE IMPORTANT LORDS FROM THROUGHOUT ENGLAND MET TO DECIDE THE FUTURE OF THE COUNTRY. THEY WERE NOT ALL READY TO CALL ARTHUR KING JUST BECAUSE HE HAD PULLED THE SWORD FROM THE STONE.
I WILL *NEVER* FOLLOW A BEARDLESS BOY!
HE PULLED THE SWORD, *KING LOT*. HE IS TO BE OUR KING AND EVEN YOURS IN FARAWAY ORKNEY.
HE DOESN'T EVEN *LOOK* LIKE A KING. I DOUBT HE WOULD MAKE A GOOD STABLE BOY!
HE'S UTHER PENDRAGON'S SON.
UTHER GAVE HIM TO ME, TRUSTING ME TO FIND THOSE WHO WOULD RAISE HIM WISELY AND SAFELY.
UTHER DIDN'T WANT HIS PRINCE AND HEIR TO BE MURDERED BY SOMEONE WHO WANTED TO BE THE NEXT KING.
HE DOES TRULY BEAR THE SEMBLANCE OF UTHER.
I PLEDGE TO ARTHUR.
LIES!
I WILL *NEVER* FOLLOW HIM !
RATHER, I WILL DEFEAT HIM *MYSELF*!
MY LIEGE.
FATHER, PLEASE, *NO*. I'M *NOT* THE KING.
I'M JUST YOUR SON.

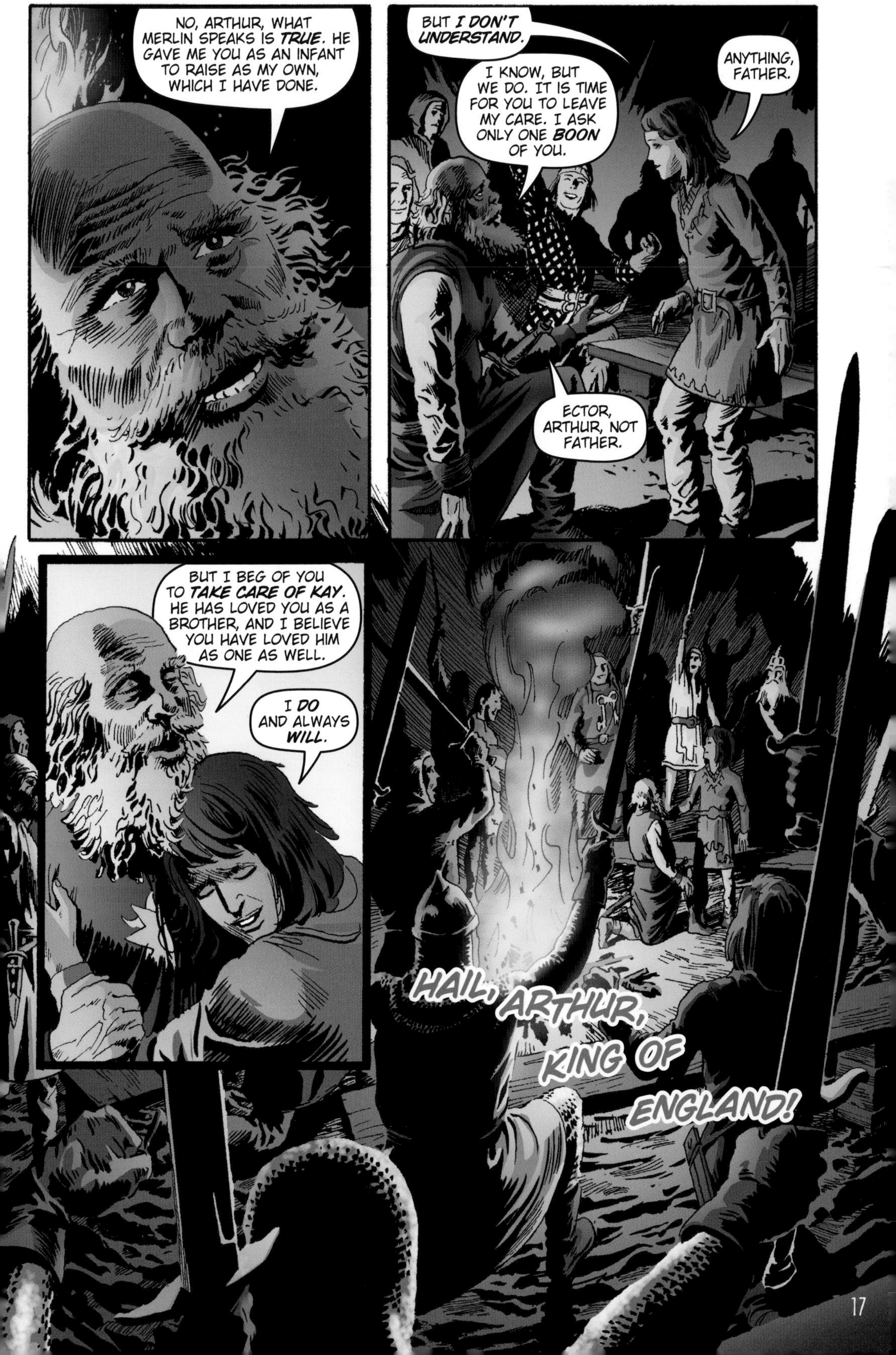
NO, ARTHUR, WHAT MERLIN SPEAKS IS TRUE. HE GAVE ME YOU AS AN INFANT TO RAISE AS MY OWN, WHICH I HAVE DONE.
BUT I DON'T UNDERSTAND.
I KNOW, BUT WE DO. IT IS TIME FOR YOU TO LEAVE MY CARE. I ASK ONLY ONE BOON OF YOU.
ANYTHING, FATHER.
ECTOR, ARTHUR, NOT FATHER.
BUT I BEG OF YOU TO TAKE CARE OF KAY. HE HAS LOVED YOU AS A BROTHER, AND I BELIEVE YOU HAVE LOVED HIM AS ONE AS WELL.
I DO AND ALWAYS WILL.
HAIL, ARTHUR, KING OF ENGLAND!

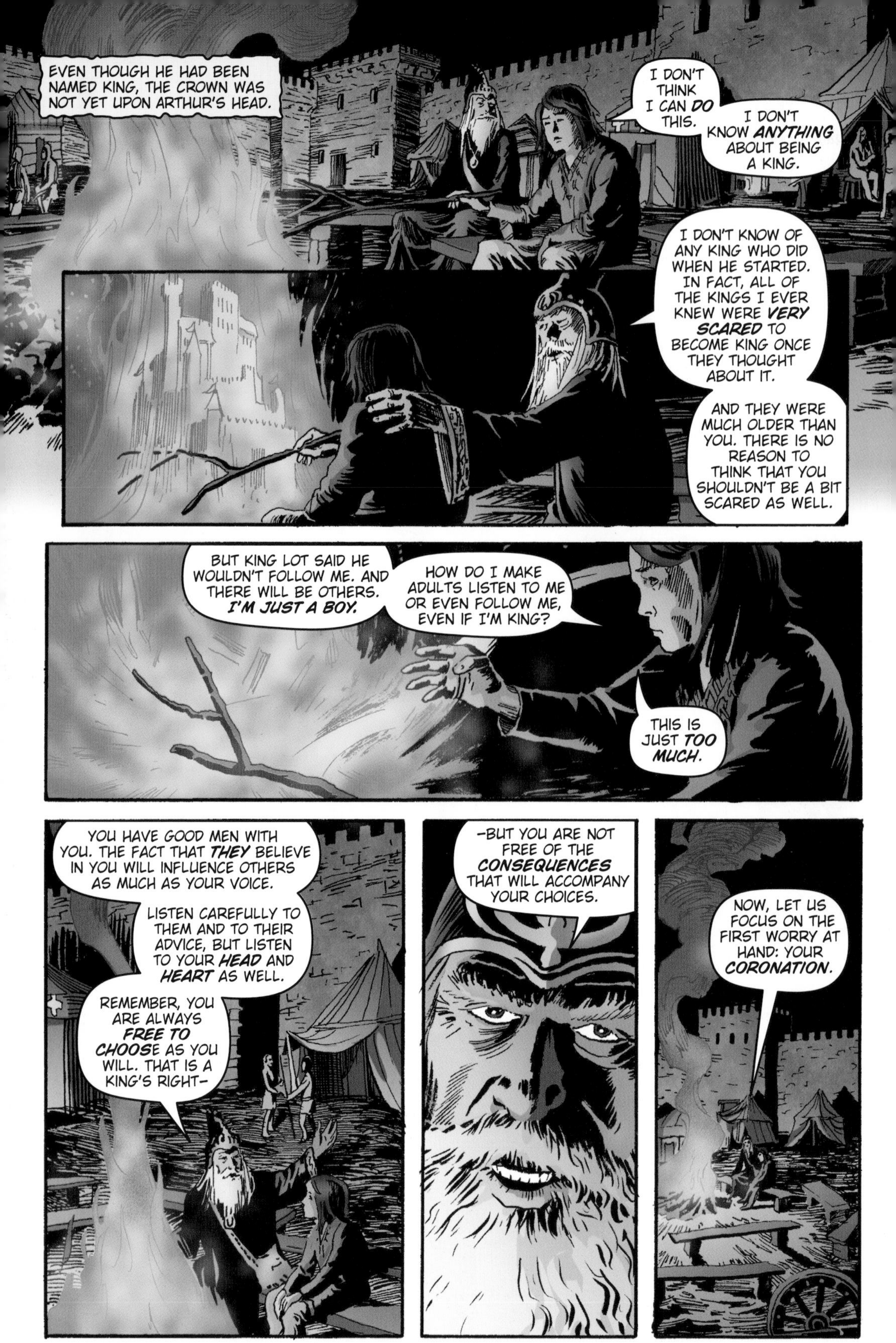

EVEN THOUGH HE HAD BEEN NAMED KING, THE CROWN WAS NOT YET UPON ARTHUR'S HEAD.
I DON'T THINK I CAN DO THIS.
I DON'T KNOW ANYTHING ABOUT BEING A KING.
I DON'T KNOW OF ANY KING WHO DID WHEN HE STARTED. IN FACT, ALL OF THE KINGS I EVER KNEW WERE VERY SCARED TO BECOME KING ONCE THEY THOUGHT ABOUT IT.
AND THEY WERE MUCH OLDER THAN YOU. THERE IS NO REASON TO THINK THAT YOU SHOULDN'T BE A BIT SCARED AS WELL.
BUT KING LOT SAID HE WOULDN'T FOLLOW ME. AND THERE WILL BE OTHERS. I'M JUST A BOY.
HOW DO I MAKE ADULTS LISTEN TO ME OR EVEN FOLLOW ME, EVEN IF I'M KING?
THIS IS JUST TOO MUCH.
YOU HAVE GOOD MEN WITH YOU. THE FACT THAT THEY BELIEVE IN YOU WILL INFLUENCE OTHERS AS MUCH AS YOUR VOICE.
LISTEN CAREFULLY TO THEM AND TO THEIR ADVICE, BUT LISTEN TO YOUR HEAD AND HEART AS WELL.
REMEMBER, YOU ARE ALWAYS FREE TO CHOOSE AS YOU WILL. THAT IS A KING'S RIGHT–
–BUT YOU ARE NOT FREE OF THE CONSEQUENCES THAT WILL ACCOMPANY YOUR CHOICES.
NOW, LET US FOCUS ON THE FIRST WORRY AT HAND: YOUR CORONATION.

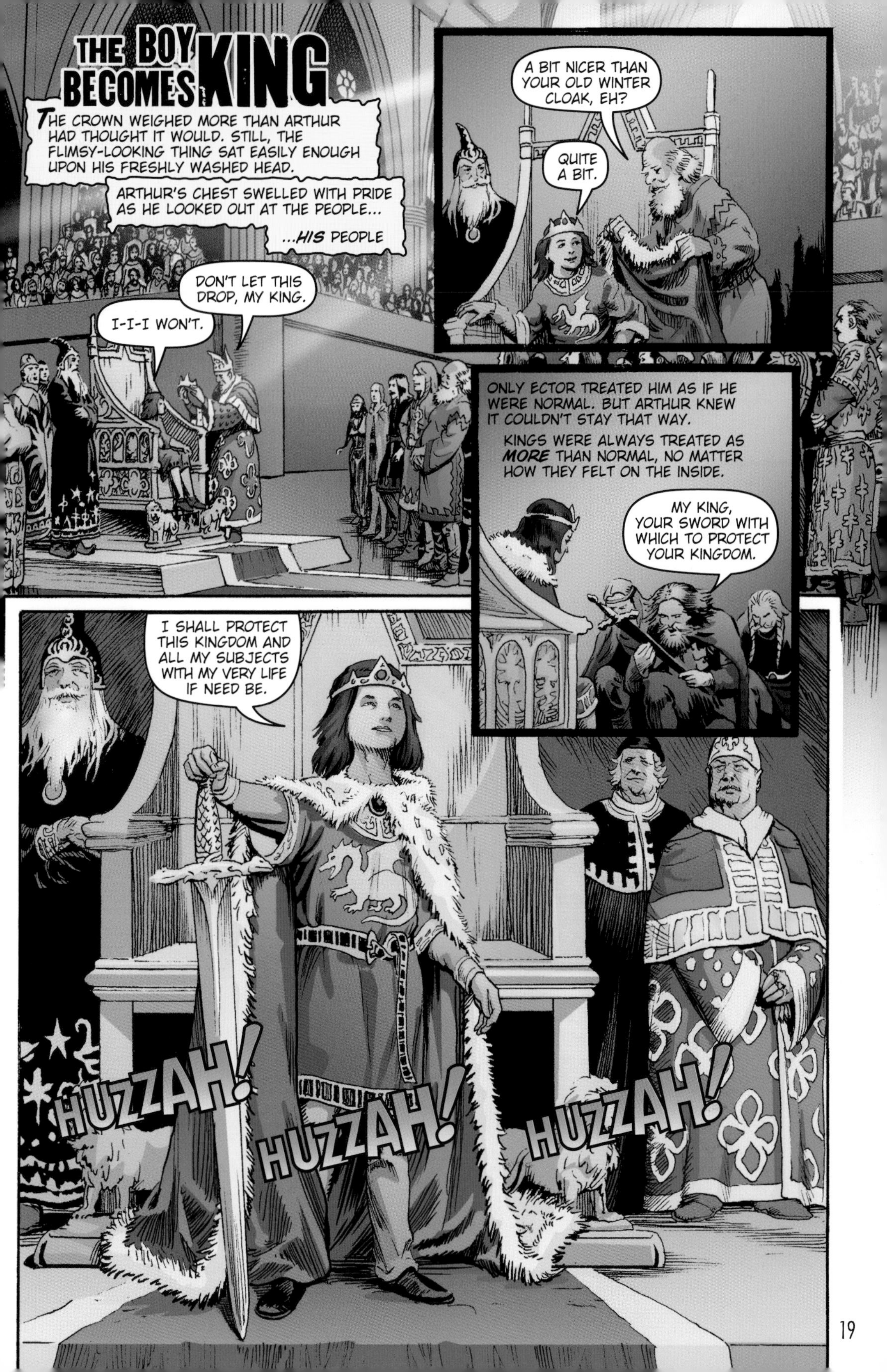
THE BOY BECOMES KING
THE CROWN WEIGHED MORE THAN ARTHUR HAD THOUGHT IT WOULD. STILL, THE FLIMSY-LOOKING THING SAT EASILY ENOUGH UPON HIS FRESHLY WASHED HEAD.
ARTHUR'S CHEST SWELLED WITH PRIDE AS HE LOOKED OUT AT THE PEOPLE...
...HIS PEOPLE
DON'T LET THIS DROP, MY KING.
I-I-I WON'T.
A BIT NICER THAN YOUR OLD WINTER CLOAK, EH?
QUITE A BIT.
ONLY ECTOR TREATED HIM AS IF HE WERE NORMAL. BUT ARTHUR KNEW IT COULDN'T STAY THAT WAY.
KINGS WERE ALWAYS TREATED AS MORE THAN NORMAL, NO MATTER HOW THEY FELT ON THE INSIDE.
MY KING, YOUR SWORD WITH WHICH TO PROTECT YOUR KINGDOM.
I SHALL PROTECT THIS KINGDOM AND ALL MY SUBJECTS WITH MY VERY LIFE IF NEED BE.
HUZZAH!
HUZZAH!
HUZZAH!

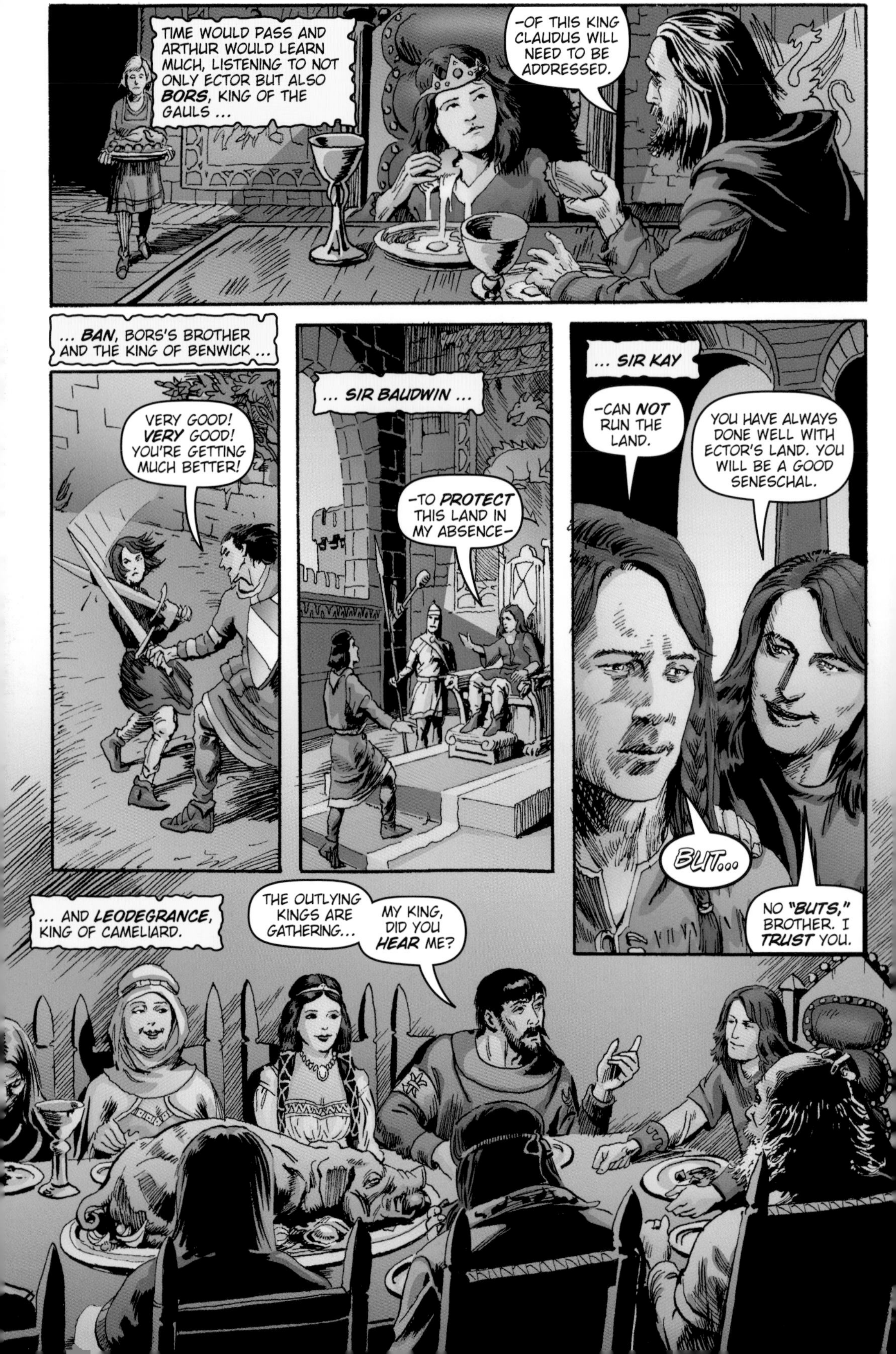
TIME WOULD PASS AND ARTHUR WOULD LEARN MUCH, LISTENING TO NOT ONLY ECTOR BUT ALSO BORS, KING OF THE GAULS ...
-OF THIS KING CLAUDUS WILL NEED TO BE ADDRESSED.
... BAN, BORS'S BROTHER AND THE KING OF BENWICK ...
VERY GOOD! VERY GOOD! YOU'RE GETTING MUCH BETTER!
... SIR BAUDWIN ...
-TO PROTECT THIS LAND IN MY ABSENCE-
... SIR KAY
-CAN NOT RUN THE LAND.
YOU HAVE ALWAYS DONE WELL WITH ECTOR'S LAND. YOU WILL BE A GOOD SENESCHAL.
BUT...
NO "BUTS," BROTHER. I TRUST YOU.
... AND LEODEGRANCE, KING OF CAMELIARD.
THE OUTLYING KINGS ARE GATHERING...
MY KING, DID YOU HEAR ME?

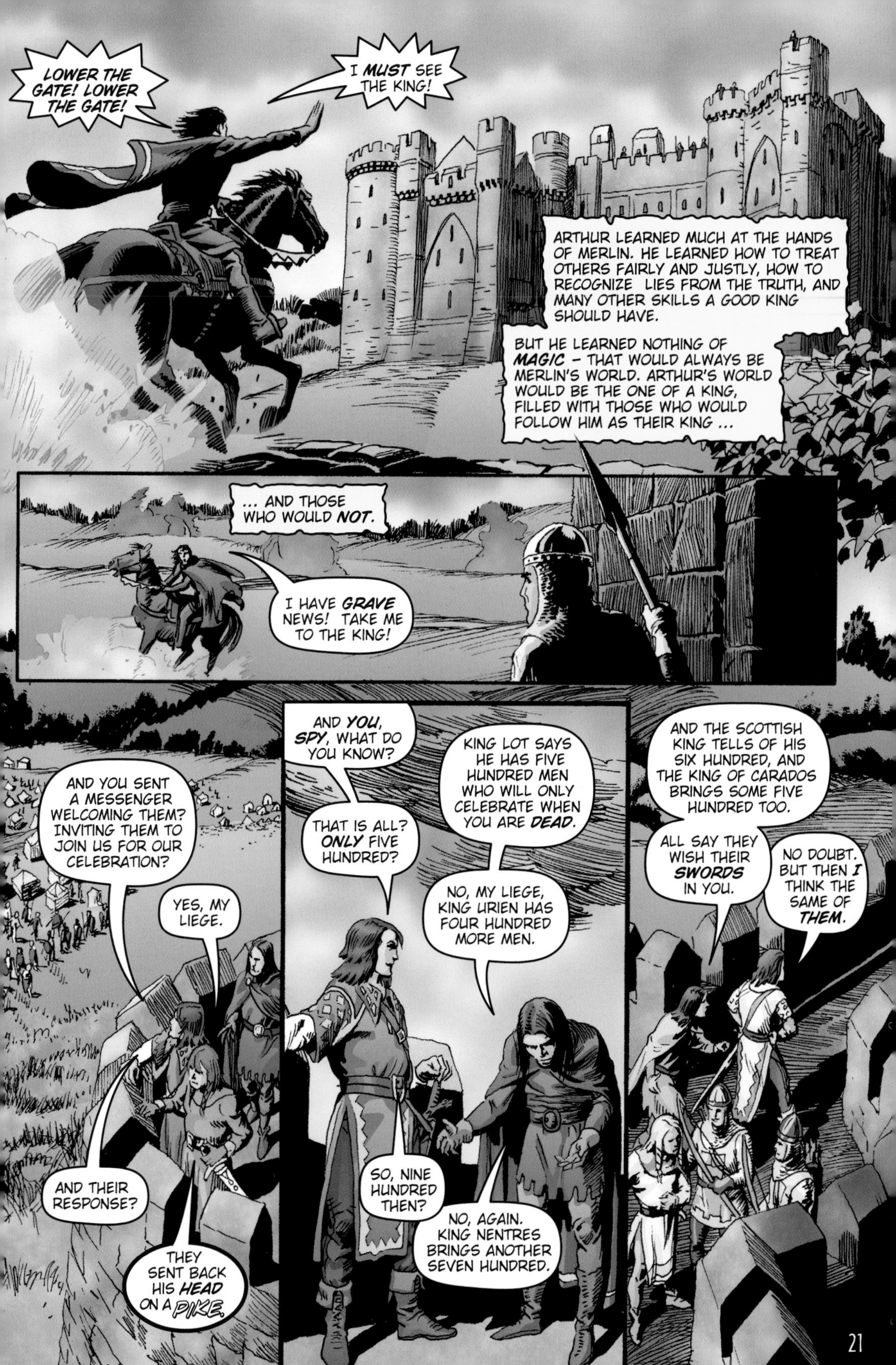
LOWER THE GATE! LOWER THE GATE!
I MUST SEE THE KING!
ARTHUR LEARNED MUCH AT THE HANDS OF MERLIN. HE LEARNED HOW TO TREAT OTHERS FAIRLY AND JUSTLY, HOW TO RECOGNIZE LIES FROM THE TRUTH, AND MANY OTHER SKILLS A GOOD KING SHOULD HAVE.
BUT HE LEARNED NOTHING OF MAGIC – THAT WOULD ALWAYS BE MERLIN'S WORLD. ARTHUR'S WORLD WOULD BE THE ONE OF A KING, FILLED WITH THOSE WHO WOULD FOLLOW HIM AS THEIR KING ...
... AND THOSE WHO WOULD NOT.
I HAVE GRAVE NEWS! TAKE ME TO THE KING!
AND YOU SENT A MESSENGER WELCOMING THEM? INVITING THEM TO JOIN US FOR OUR CELEBRATION?
YES, MY LIEGE.
AND THEIR RESPONSE?
THEY SENT BACK HIS HEAD ON A PIKE.
AND YOU, SPY, WHAT DO YOU KNOW?
KING LOT SAYS HE HAS FIVE HUNDRED MEN WHO WILL ONLY CELEBRATE WHEN YOU ARE DEAD.
THAT IS ALL? ONLY FIVE HUNDRED?
NO, MY LIEGE, KING URIEN HAS FOUR HUNDRED MORE MEN.
SO, NINE HUNDRED THEN?
NO, AGAIN. KING NENTRES BRINGS ANOTHER SEVEN HUNDRED.
AND THE SCOTTISH KING TELLS OF HIS SIX HUNDRED, AND THE KING OF CARADOS BRINGS SOME FIVE HUNDRED TOO.
ALL SAY THEY WISH THEIR SWORDS IN YOU.
NO DOUBT. BUT THEN I THINK THE SAME OF THEM.

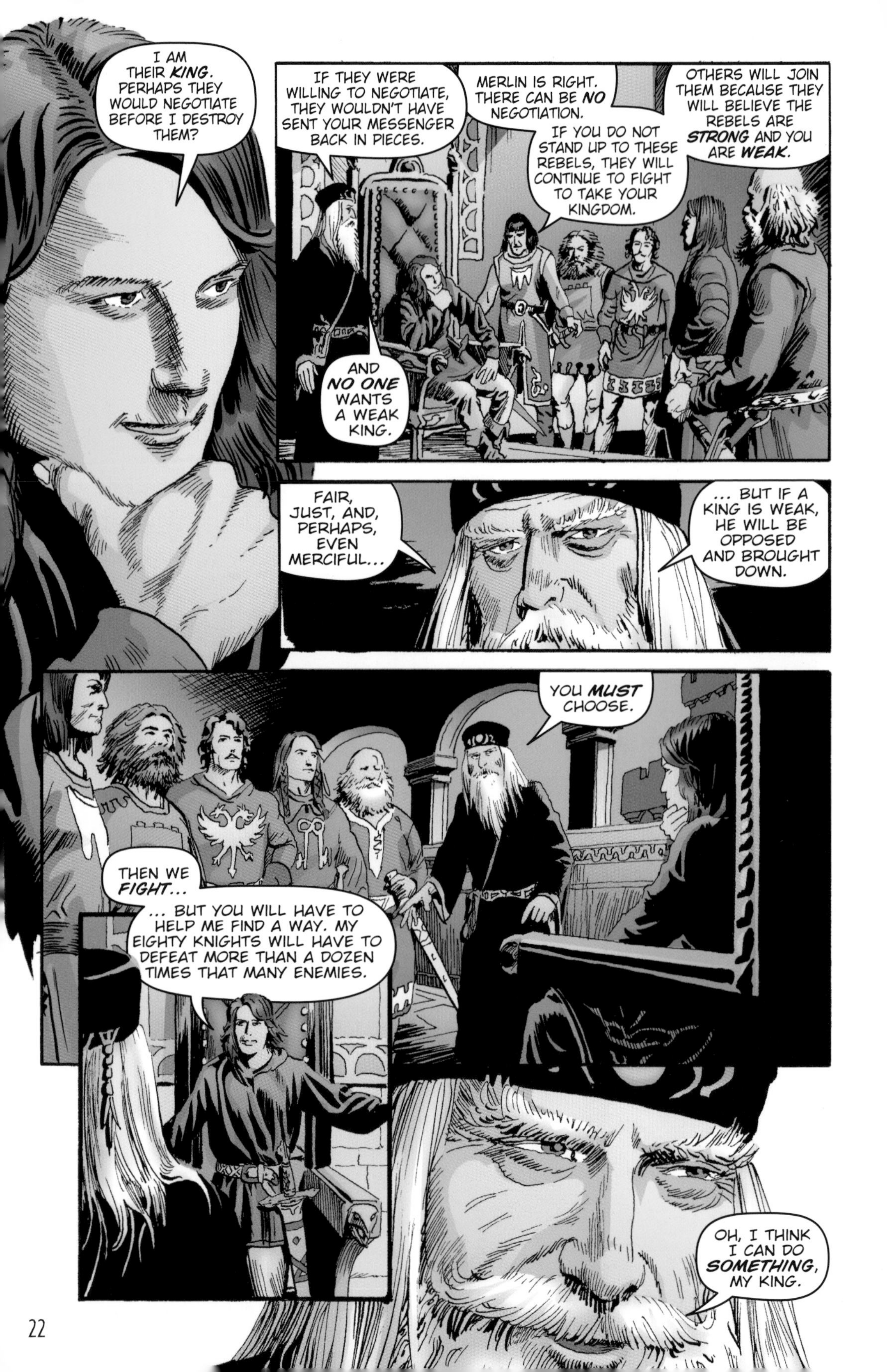
I AM THEIR KING. PERHAPS THEY WOULD NEGOTIATE BEFORE I DESTROY THEM?
IF THEY WERE WILLING TO NEGOTIATE, THEY WOULDN'T HAVE SENT YOUR MESSENGER BACK IN PIECES.
AND NO ONE WANTS A WEAK KING.
MERLIN IS RIGHT. THERE CAN BE NO NEGOTIATION.
IF YOU DO NOT STAND UP TO THESE REBELS, THEY WILL CONTINUE TO FIGHT TO TAKE YOUR KINGDOM.
OTHERS WILL JOIN THEM BECAUSE THEY WILL BELIEVE THE REBELS ARE STRONG AND YOU ARE WEAK.
FAIR, JUST, AND, PERHAPS, EVEN MERCIFUL...
... BUT IF A KING IS WEAK, HE WILL BE OPPOSED AND BROUGHT DOWN.
YOU MUST CHOOSE.
THEN WE FIGHT...
... BUT YOU WILL HAVE TO HELP ME FIND A WAY. MY EIGHTY KNIGHTS WILL HAVE TO DEFEAT MORE THAN A DOZEN TIMES THAT MANY ENEMIES.
OH, I THINK I CAN DO SOMETHING, MY KING.

THE LESSON TAUGHT TO KING LOT

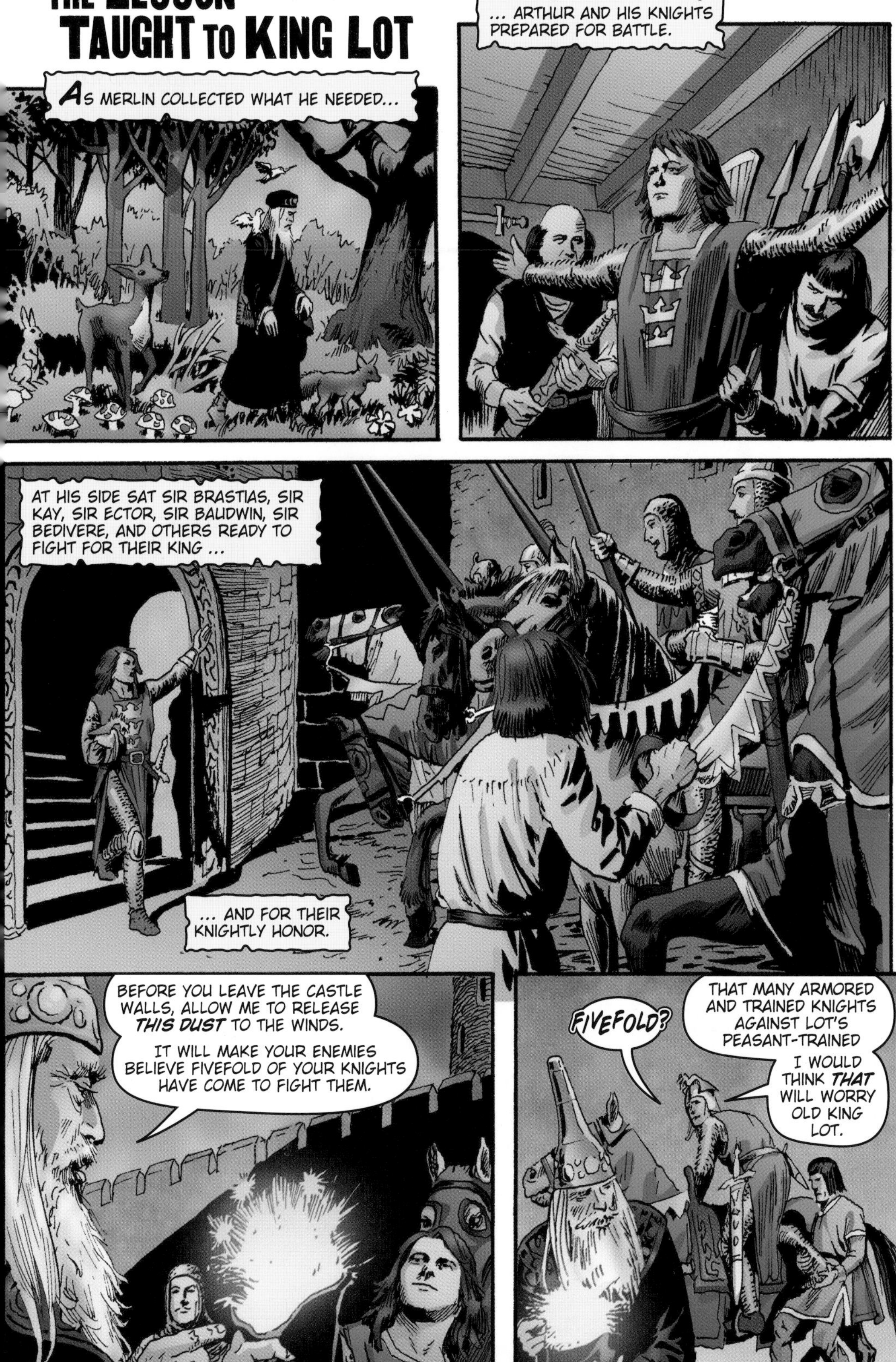

AS MERLIN COLLECTED WHAT HE NEEDED...
... ARTHUR AND HIS KNIGHTS PREPARED FOR BATTLE.
AT HIS SIDE SAT SIR BRASTIAS, SIR KAY, SIR ECTOR, SIR BAUDWIN, SIR BEDIVERE, AND OTHERS READY TO FIGHT FOR THEIR KING ...
... AND FOR THEIR KNIGHTLY HONOR.
BEFORE YOU LEAVE THE CASTLE WALLS, ALLOW ME TO RELEASE THIS DUST TO THE WINDS.
IT WILL MAKE YOUR ENEMIES BELIEVE FIVEFOLD OF YOUR KNIGHTS HAVE COME TO FIGHT THEM.
FIVEFOLD?
THAT MANY ARMORED AND TRAINED KNIGHTS AGAINST LOT'S PEASANT-TRAINED
I WOULD THINK THAT WILL WORRY OLD KING LOT.

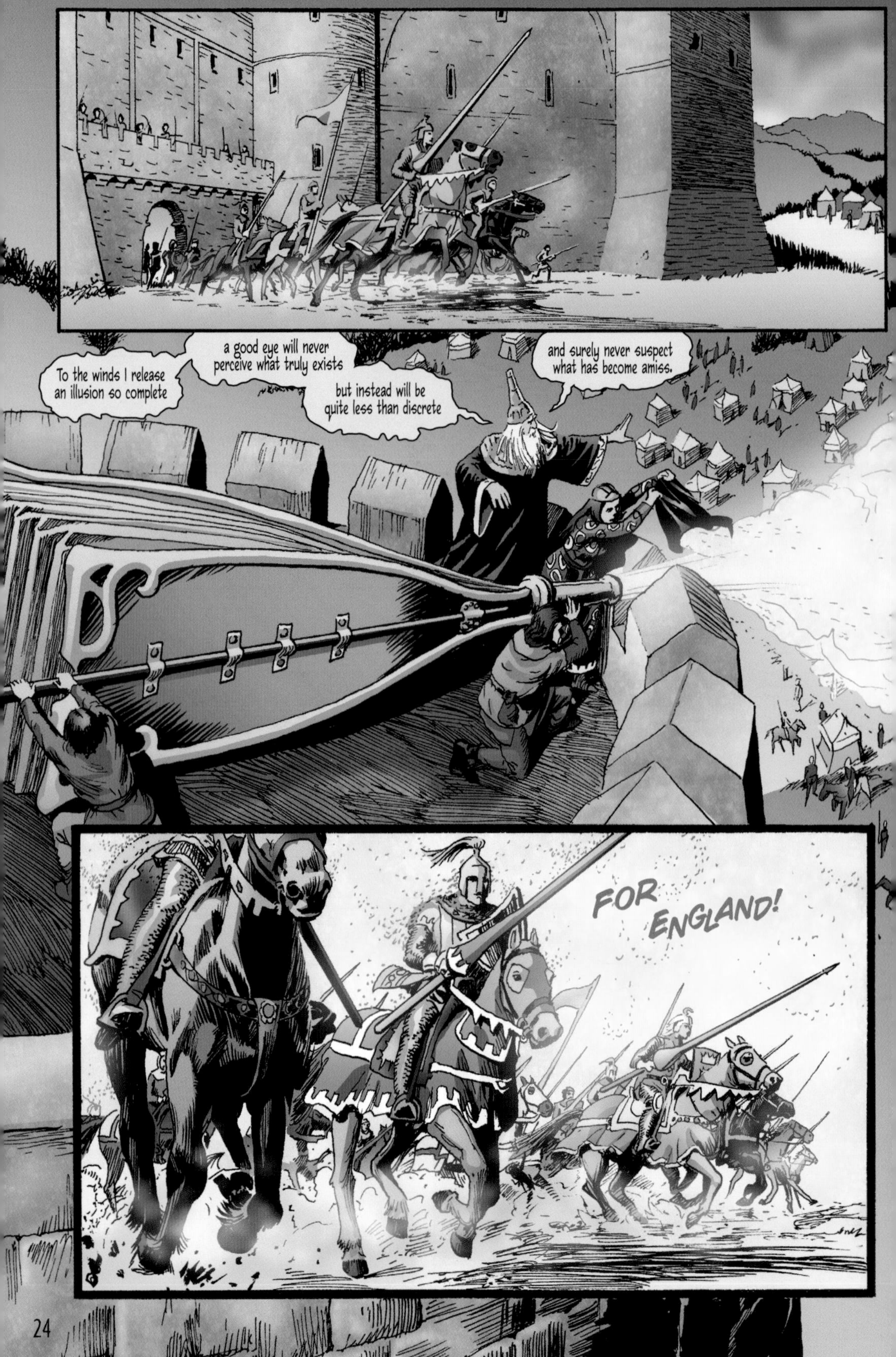
To the winds I release an illusion so complete
a good eye will never perceive what truly exists
but instead will be quite less than discrete
and surely never suspect what has become amiss.
FOR ENGLAND!

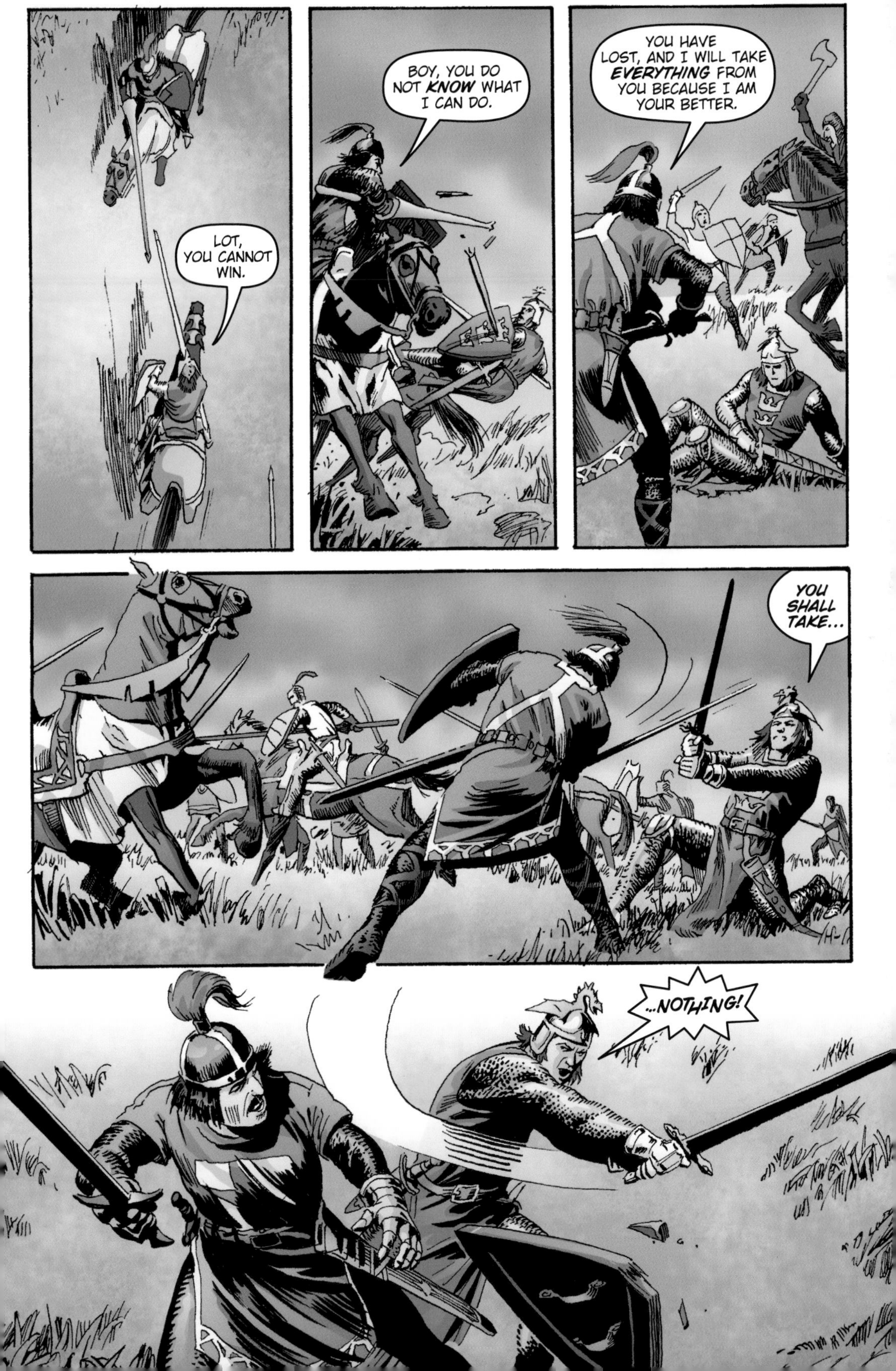
LOT, YOU CANNOT WIN.
BOY, YOU DO NOT KNOW WHAT I CAN DO.
YOU HAVE LOST, AND I WILL TAKE EVERYTHING FROM YOU BECAUSE I AM YOUR BETTER.
YOU SHALL TAKE...
...NOTHING!

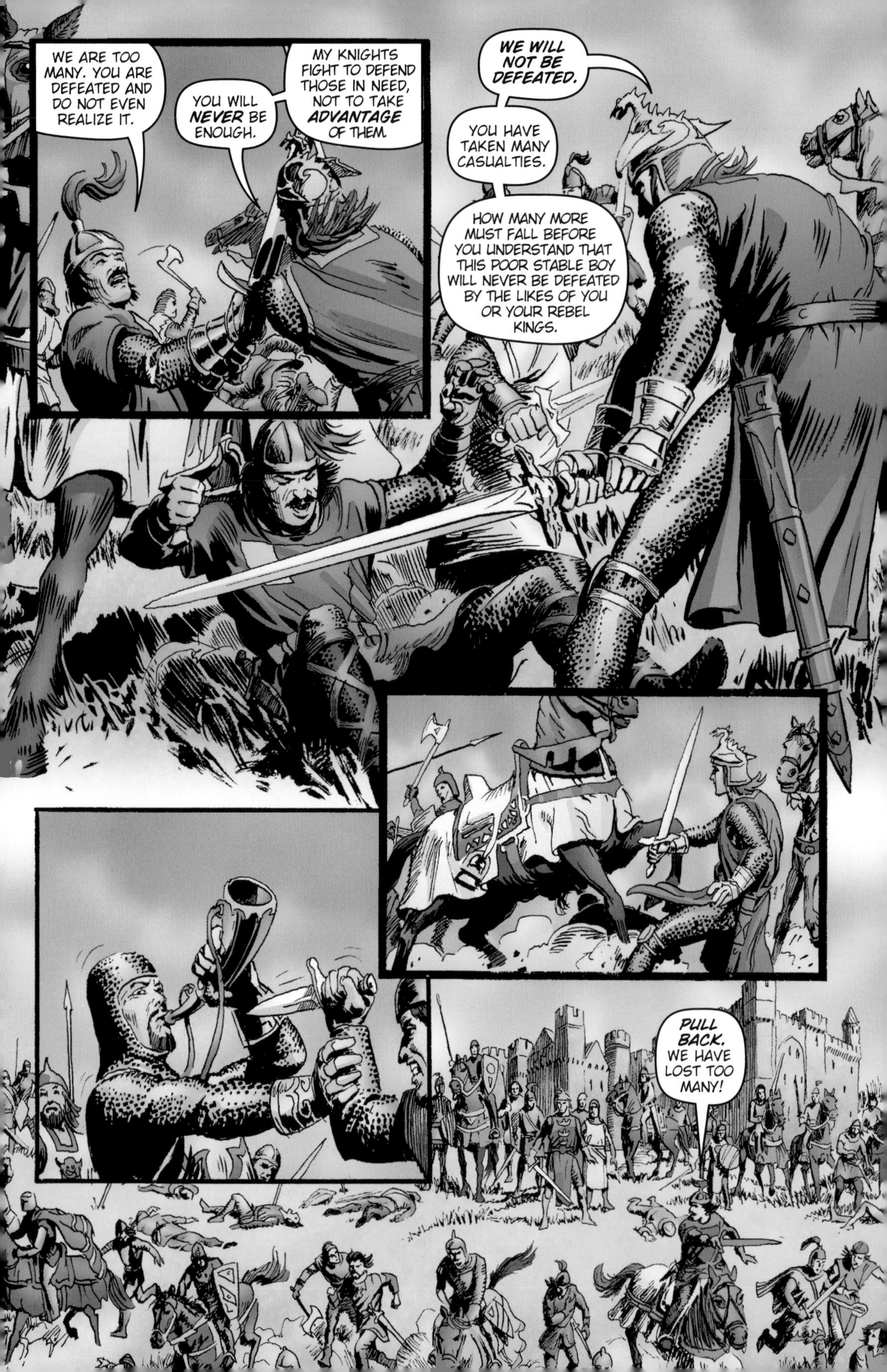
WE ARE TOO MANY. YOU ARE DEFEATED AND DO NOT EVEN REALIZE IT.
YOU WILL NEVER BE ENOUGH.
MY KNIGHTS FIGHT TO DEFEND THOSE IN NEED, NOT TO TAKE ADVANTAGE OF THEM.
WE WILL NOT BE DEFEATED.
YOU HAVE TAKEN MANY CASUALTIES.
HOW MANY MORE MUST FALL BEFORE YOU UNDERSTAND THAT THIS POOR STABLE BOY WILL NEVER BE DEFEATED BY THE LIKES OF YOU OR YOUR REBEL KINGS.
PULL BACK. WE HAVE LOST TOO MANY!

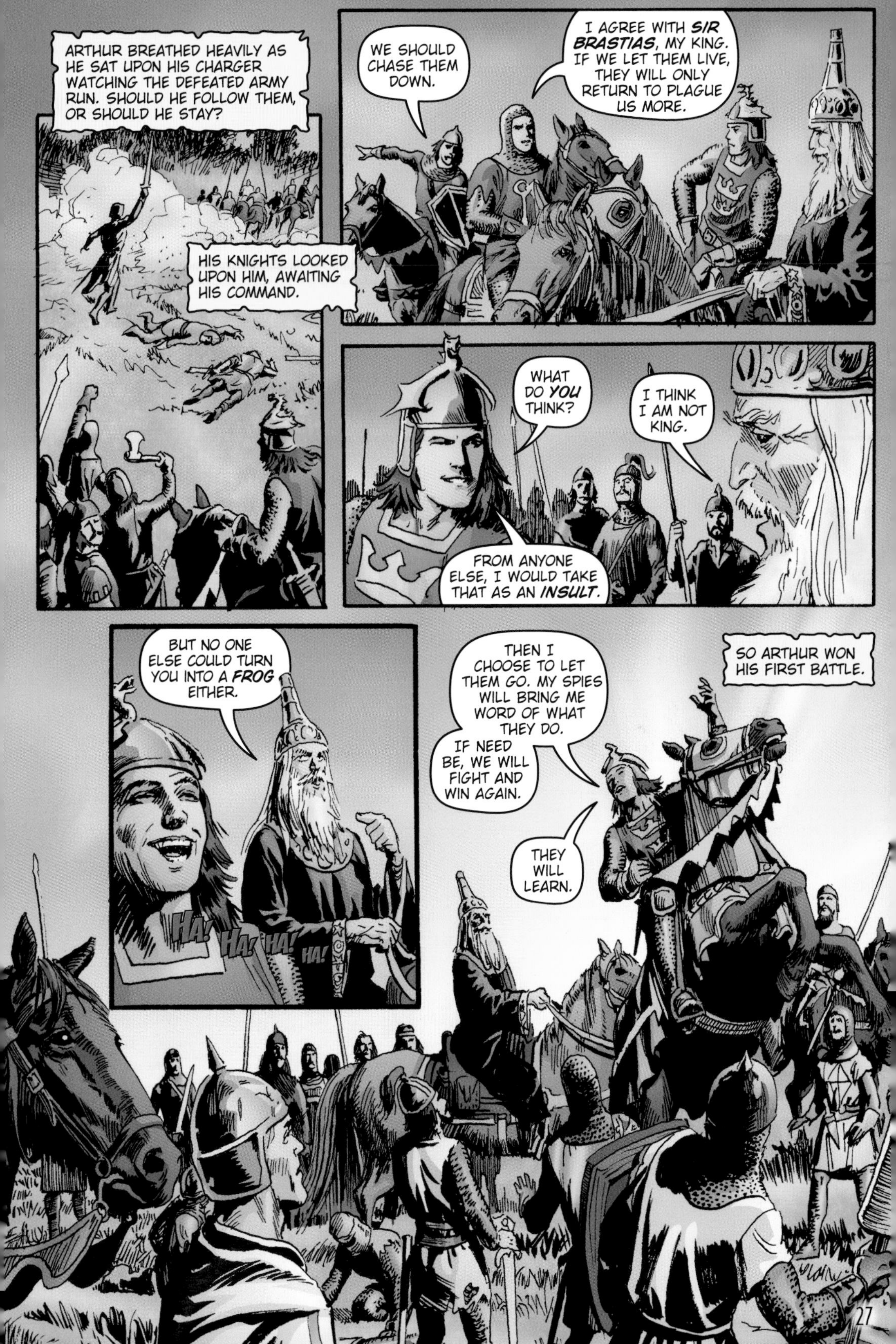

ARTHUR BREATHED HEAVILY AS HE SAT UPON HIS CHARGER WATCHING THE DEFEATED ARMY RUN. SHOULD HE FOLLOW THEM, OR SHOULD HE STAY?
HIS KNIGHTS LOOKED UPON HIM, AWAITING HIS COMMAND.
WE SHOULD CHASE THEM DOWN.
I AGREE WITH SIR BRASTIAS, MY KING. IF WE LET THEM LIVE, THEY WILL ONLY RETURN TO PLAGUE US MORE.
WHAT DO YOU THINK?
I THINK I AM NOT KING.
FROM ANYONE ELSE, I WOULD TAKE THAT AS AN INSULT.
BUT NO ONE ELSE COULD TURN YOU INTO A FROG EITHER.
HA! HA! HA! HA!
THEN I CHOOSE TO LET THEM GO. MY SPIES WILL BRING ME WORD OF WHAT THEY DO.
IF NEED BE, WE WILL FIGHT AND WIN AGAIN.
THEY WILL LEARN.
SO ARTHUR WON HIS FIRST BATTLE.

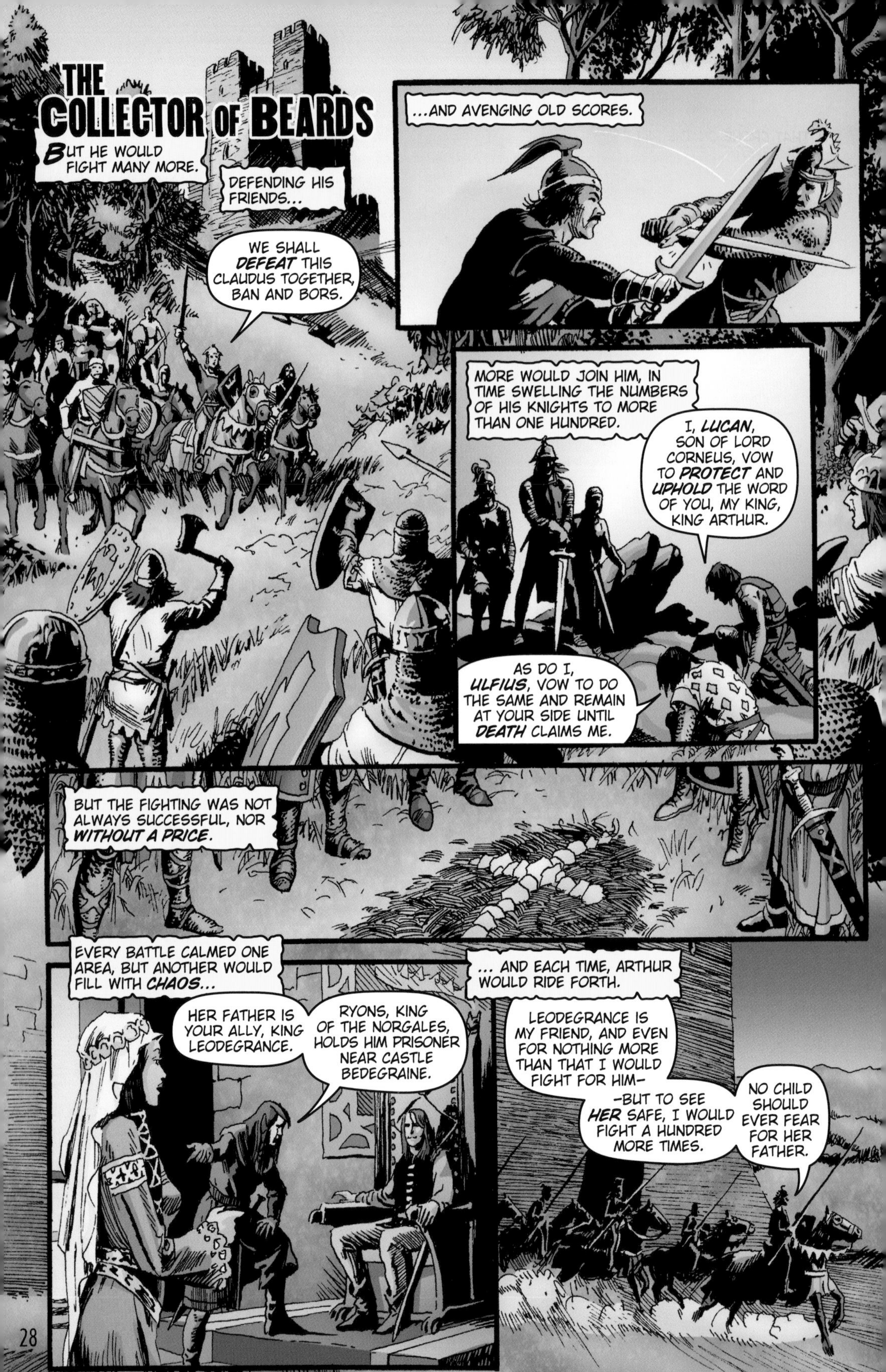
THE COLLECTOR OF BEARDS
BUT HE WOULD FIGHT MANY MORE.
DEFENDING HIS FRIENDS...
WE SHALL DEFEAT THIS CLAUDUS TOGETHER, BAN AND BORS.
...AND AVENGING OLD SCORES.
MORE WOULD JOIN HIM, IN TIME SWELLING THE NUMBERS OF HIS KNIGHTS TO MORE THAN ONE HUNDRED.
I, LUCAN, SON OF LORD CORNEUS, VOW TO PROTECT AND UPHOLD THE WORD OF YOU, MY KING, KING ARTHUR.
AS DO I, ULFIUS, VOW TO DO THE SAME AND REMAIN AT YOUR SIDE UNTIL DEATH CLAIMS ME.
BUT THE FIGHTING WAS NOT ALWAYS SUCCESSFUL, NOR WITHOUT A PRICE.
EVERY BATTLE CALMED ONE AREA, BUT ANOTHER WOULD FILL WITH CHAOS...
HER FATHER IS YOUR ALLY, KING LEODEGRANCE.
RYONS, KING OF THE NORGALES, HOLDS HIM PRISONER NEAR CASTLE BEDEGRAINE.
... AND EACH TIME, ARTHUR WOULD RIDE FORTH.
LEODEGRANCE IS MY FRIEND, AND EVEN FOR NOTHING MORE THAN THAT I WOULD FIGHT FOR HIM-
-BUT TO SEE HER SAFE, I WOULD FIGHT A HUNDRED MORE TIMES.
NO CHILD SHOULD EVER FEAR FOR HER FATHER.

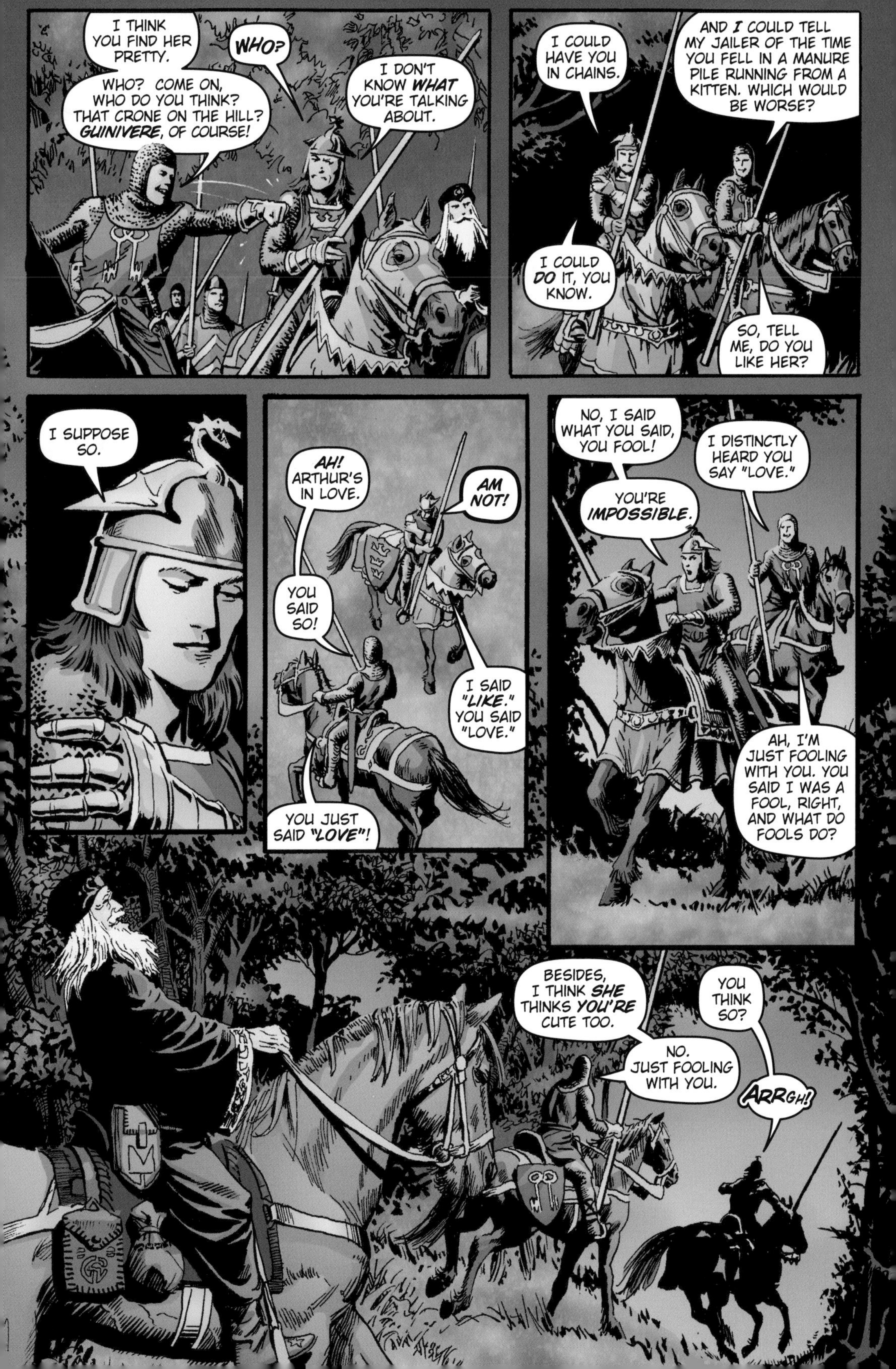
I THINK YOU FIND HER PRETTY.
WHO?
WHO? COME ON, WHO DO YOU THINK? THAT CRONE ON THE HILL? GUINIVERE, OF COURSE!
I DON'T KNOW WHAT YOU'RE TALKING ABOUT.
I COULD HAVE YOU IN CHAINS.
AND I COULD TELL MY JAILER OF THE TIME YOU FELL IN A MANURE PILE RUNNING FROM A KITTEN. WHICH WOULD BE WORSE?
I COULD DO IT, YOU KNOW.
SO, TELL ME, DO YOU LIKE HER?
I SUPPOSE SO.
AH! ARTHUR'S IN LOVE.
AM NOT!
YOU SAID SO!
I SAID "LIKE." YOU SAID "LOVE."
YOU JUST SAID "LOVE"!
NO, I SAID WHAT YOU SAID, YOU FOOL!
I DISTINCTLY HEARD YOU SAY "LOVE."
YOU'RE IMPOSSIBLE.
AH, I'M JUST FOOLING WITH YOU. YOU SAID I WAS A FOOL, RIGHT, AND WHAT DO FOOLS DO?
BESIDES, I THINK SHE THINKS YOU'RE CUTE TOO.
YOU THINK SO?
NO. JUST FOOLING WITH YOU.
ARRGH!

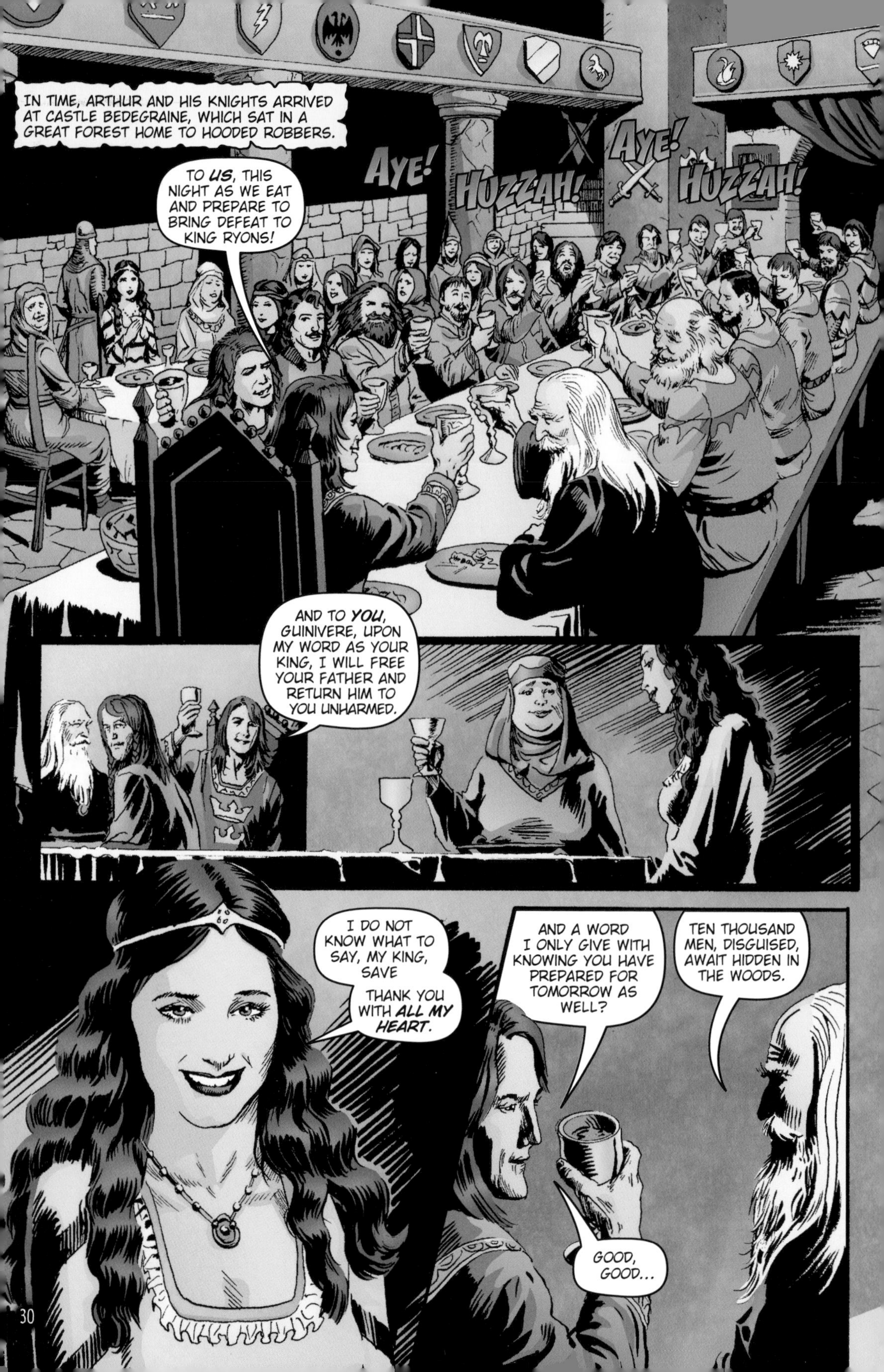
IN TIME, ARTHUR AND HIS KNIGHTS ARRIVED AT CASTLE BEDEGRAINE, WHICH SAT IN A GREAT FOREST HOME TO HOODED ROBBERS.
TO US, THIS NIGHT AS WE EAT AND PREPARE TO BRING DEFEAT TO KING RYONS!
AYE!
HUZZAH!
AYE!
HUZZAH!
AND TO YOU, GUINIVERE, UPON MY WORD AS YOUR KING, I WILL FREE YOUR FATHER AND RETURN HIM TO YOU UNHARMED.
I DO NOT KNOW WHAT TO SAY, MY KING, SAVE
THANK YOU WITH ALL MY HEART.
AND A WORD I ONLY GIVE WITH KNOWING YOU HAVE PREPARED FOR TOMORROW AS WELL?
TEN THOUSAND MEN, DISGUISED, AWAIT HIDDEN IN THE WOODS.
GOOD, GOOD...

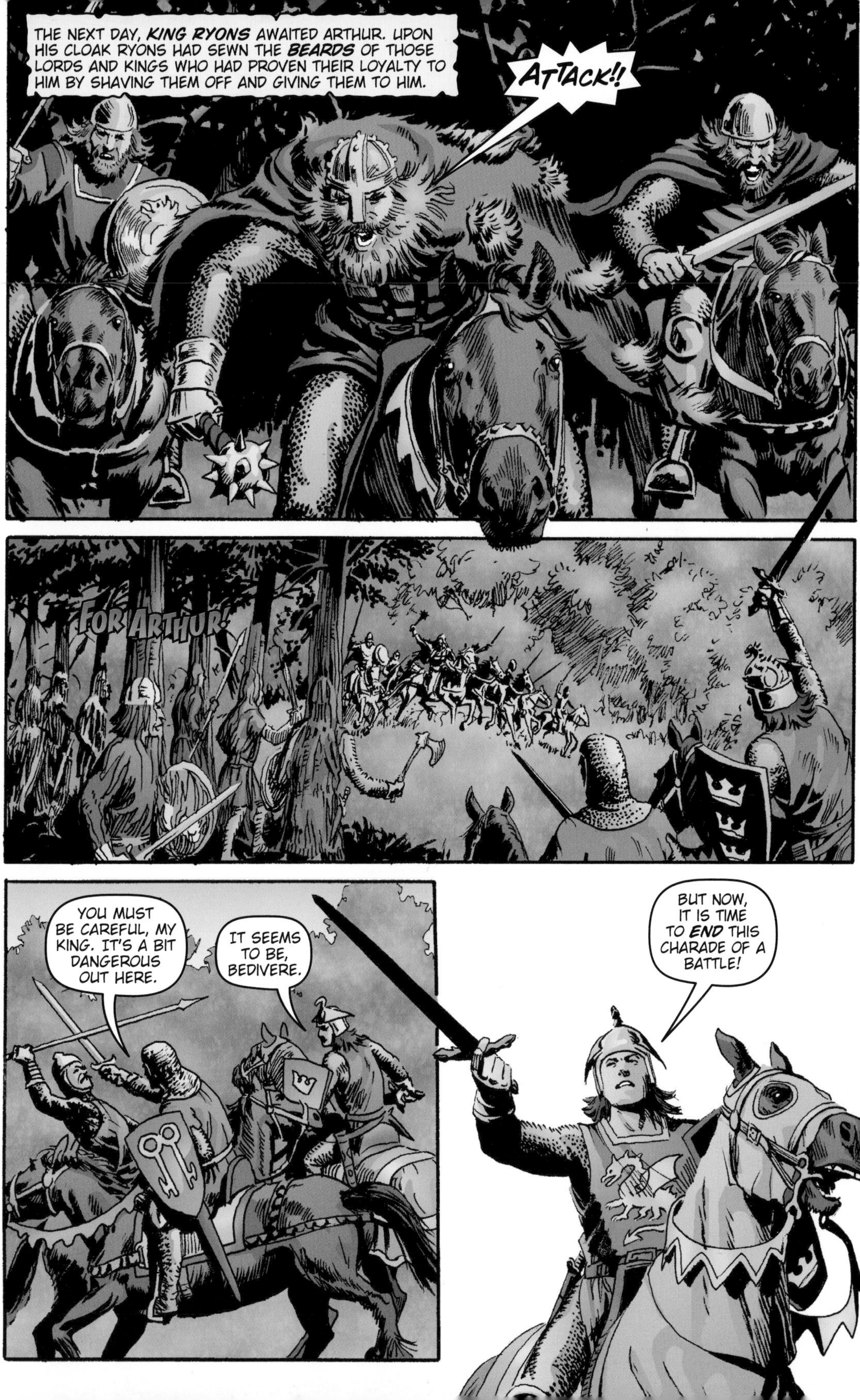
THE NEXT DAY, KING RYONS AWAITED ARTHUR. UPON HIS CLOAK RYONS HAD SEWN THE BEARDS OF THOSE LORDS AND KINGS WHO HAD PROVEN THEIR LOYALTY TO HIM BY SHAVING THEM OFF AND GIVING THEM TO HIM.
ATTACK!!
FOR ARTHUR!
YOU MUST BE CAREFUL, MY KING. IT'S A BIT DANGEROUS OUT HERE.
IT SEEMS TO BE, BEDIVERE.
BUT NOW, IT IS TIME TO END THIS CHARADE OF A BATTLE!

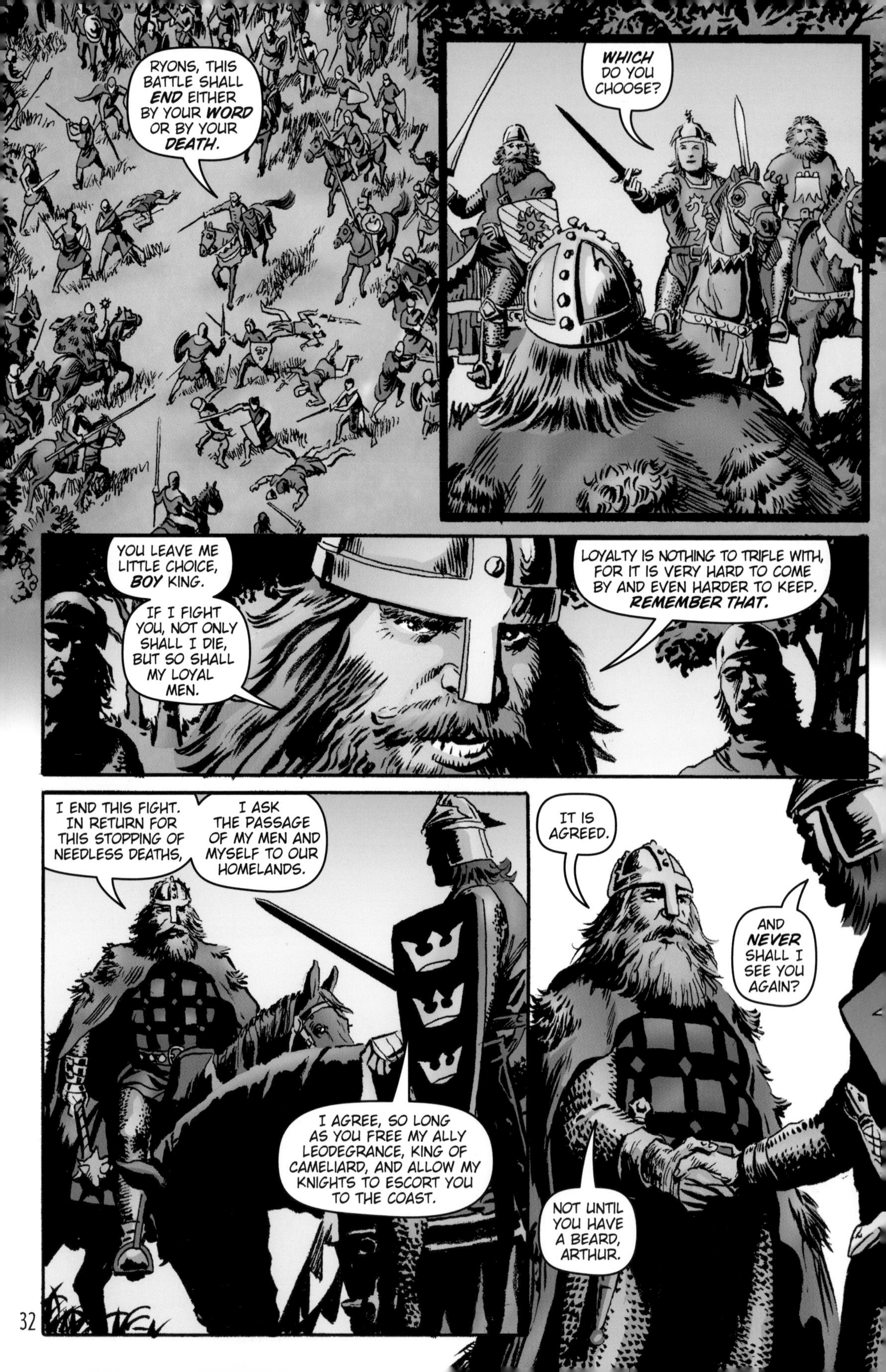

RYONS, THIS BATTLE SHALL END EITHER BY YOUR WORD OR BY YOUR DEATH.
WHICH DO YOU CHOOSE?
YOU LEAVE ME LITTLE CHOICE, BOY KING.
IF I FIGHT YOU, NOT ONLY SHALL I DIE, BUT SO SHALL MY LOYAL MEN.
LOYALTY IS NOTHING TO TRIFLE WITH, FOR IT IS VERY HARD TO COME BY AND EVEN HARDER TO KEEP. REMEMBER THAT.
I END THIS FIGHT. IN RETURN FOR THIS STOPPING OF NEEDLESS DEATHS,
I ASK THE PASSAGE OF MY MEN AND MYSELF TO OUR HOMELANDS.
I AGREE, SO LONG AS YOU FREE MY ALLY LEODEGRANCE, KING OF CAMELIARD, AND ALLOW MY KNIGHTS TO ESCORT YOU TO THE COAST.
IT IS AGREED.
AND NEVER SHALL I SEE YOU AGAIN?
NOT UNTIL YOU HAVE A BEARD, ARTHUR.

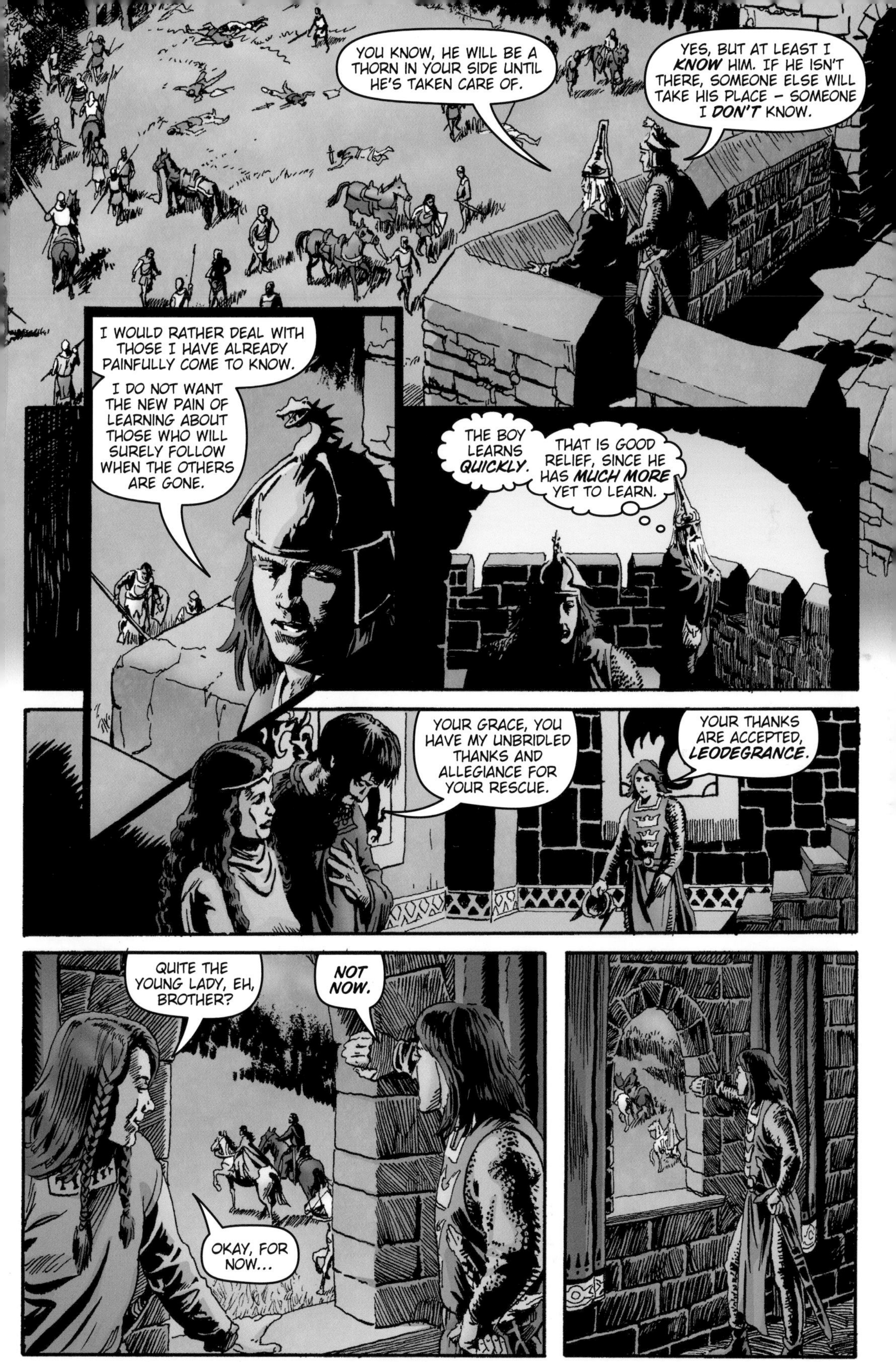
YOU KNOW, HE WILL BE A THORN IN YOUR SIDE UNTIL HE'S TAKEN CARE OF.
YES, BUT AT LEAST I **KNOW** HIM. IF HE ISN'T THERE, SOMEONE ELSE WILL TAKE HIS PLACE – SOMEONE I **DON'T** KNOW.
I WOULD RATHER DEAL WITH THOSE I HAVE ALREADY PAINFULLY COME TO KNOW.
I DO NOT WANT THE NEW PAIN OF LEARNING ABOUT THOSE WHO WILL SURELY FOLLOW WHEN THE OTHERS ARE GONE.
THE BOY LEARNS **QUICKLY**.
THAT IS GOOD RELIEF, SINCE HE HAS **MUCH MORE** YET TO LEARN.
YOUR GRACE, YOU HAVE MY UNBRIDLED THANKS AND ALLEGIANCE FOR YOUR RESCUE.
YOUR THANKS ARE ACCEPTED, **LEODEGRANCE**.
QUITE THE YOUNG LADY, EH, BROTHER?
NOT NOW.
OKAY, FOR NOW...

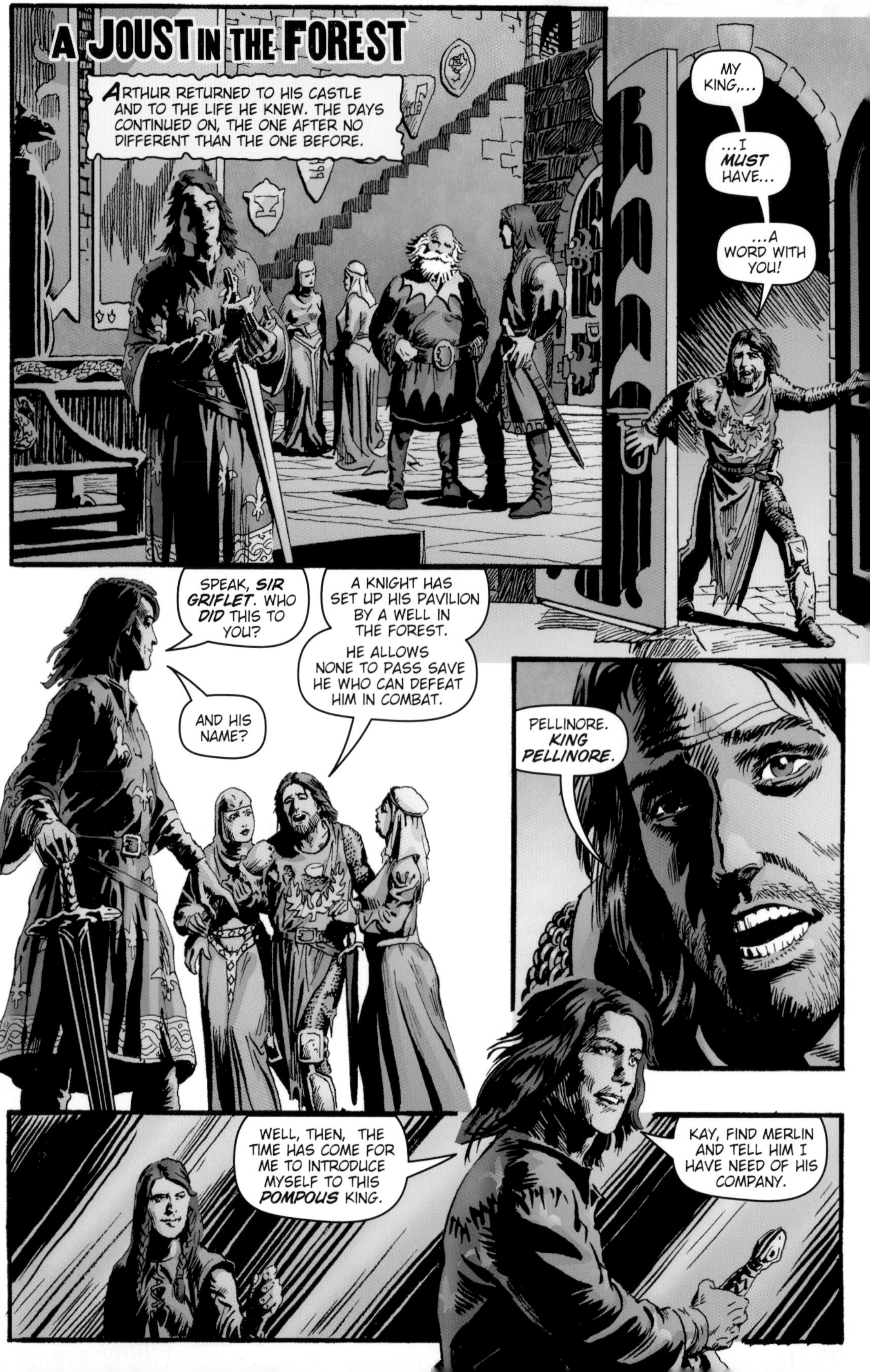
A JOUST IN THE FOREST
ARTHUR RETURNED TO HIS CASTLE AND TO THE LIFE HE KNEW. THE DAYS CONTINUED ON, THE ONE AFTER NO DIFFERENT THAN THE ONE BEFORE.
MY KING,...
...I MUST HAVE...
...A WORD WITH YOU!
SPEAK, SIR GRIFLET. WHO DID THIS TO YOU?
A KNIGHT HAS SET UP HIS PAVILION BY A WELL IN THE FOREST.
HE ALLOWS NONE TO PASS SAVE HE WHO CAN DEFEAT HIM IN COMBAT.
AND HIS NAME?
PELLINORE. KING PELLINORE.
WELL, THEN, THE TIME HAS COME FOR ME TO INTRODUCE MYSELF TO THIS POMPOUS KING.
KAY, FIND MERLIN AND TELL HIM I HAVE NEED OF HIS COMPANY.

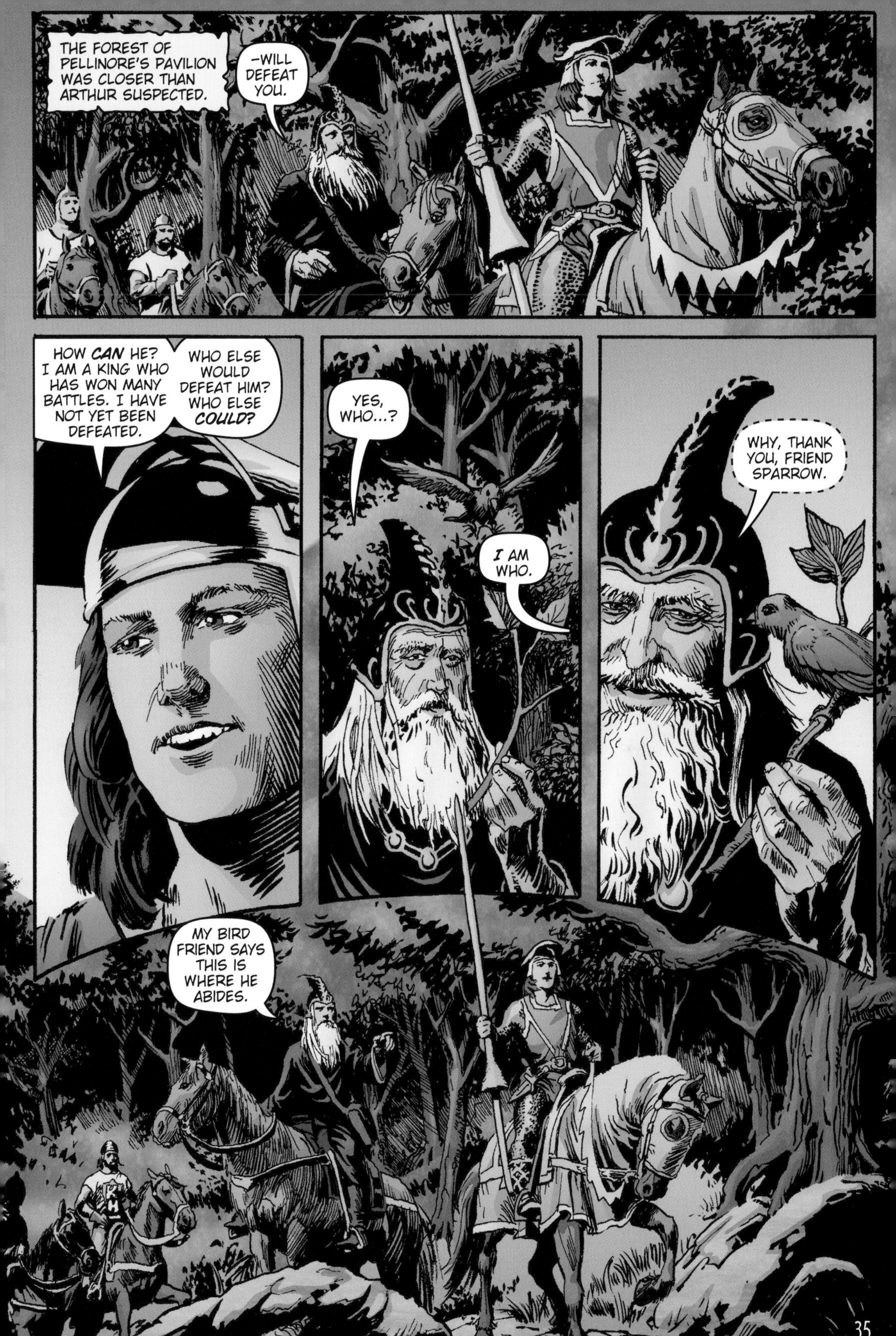
THE FOREST OF PELLINORE'S PAVILION WAS CLOSER THAN ARTHUR SUSPECTED.
—WILL DEFEAT YOU.
HOW CAN HE? I AM A KING WHO HAS WON MANY BATTLES. I HAVE NOT YET BEEN DEFEATED.
WHO ELSE WOULD DEFEAT HIM? WHO ELSE COULD?
YES, WHO...?
I AM WHO.
WHY, THANK YOU, FRIEND SPARROW.
MY BIRD FRIEND SAYS THIS IS WHERE HE ABIDES.

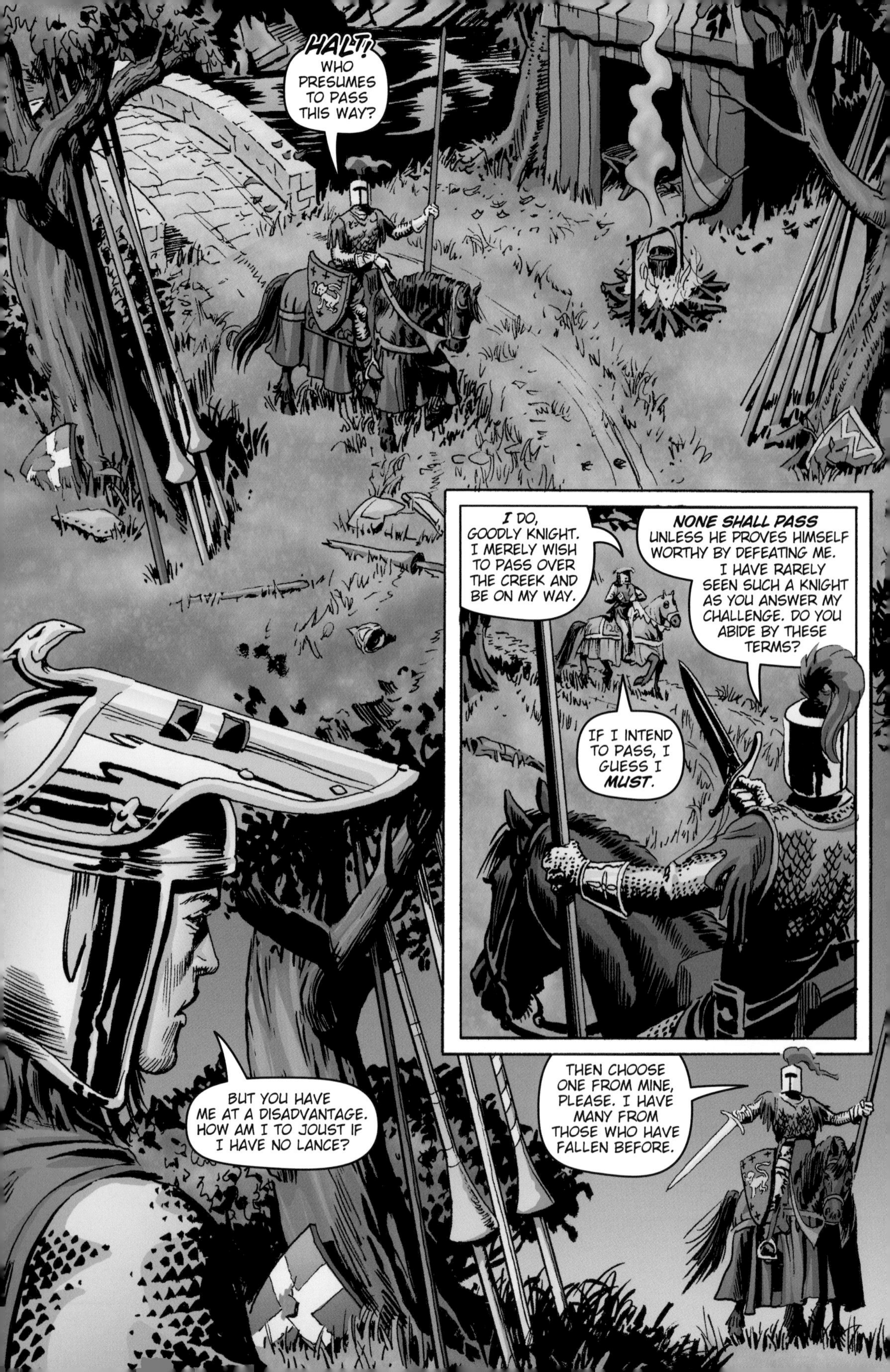
HALT! WHO PRESUMES TO PASS THIS WAY?
I DO, GOODLY KNIGHT. I MERELY WISH TO PASS OVER THE CREEK AND BE ON MY WAY.
NONE SHALL PASS UNLESS HE PROVES HIMSELF WORTHY BY DEFEATING ME. I HAVE RARELY SEEN SUCH A KNIGHT AS YOU ANSWER MY CHALLENGE. DO YOU ABIDE BY THESE TERMS?
IF I INTEND TO PASS, I GUESS I MUST.
BUT YOU HAVE ME AT A DISADVANTAGE. HOW AM I TO JOUST IF I HAVE NO LANCE?
THEN CHOOSE ONE FROM MINE, PLEASE. I HAVE MANY FROM THOSE WHO HAVE FALLEN BEFORE.

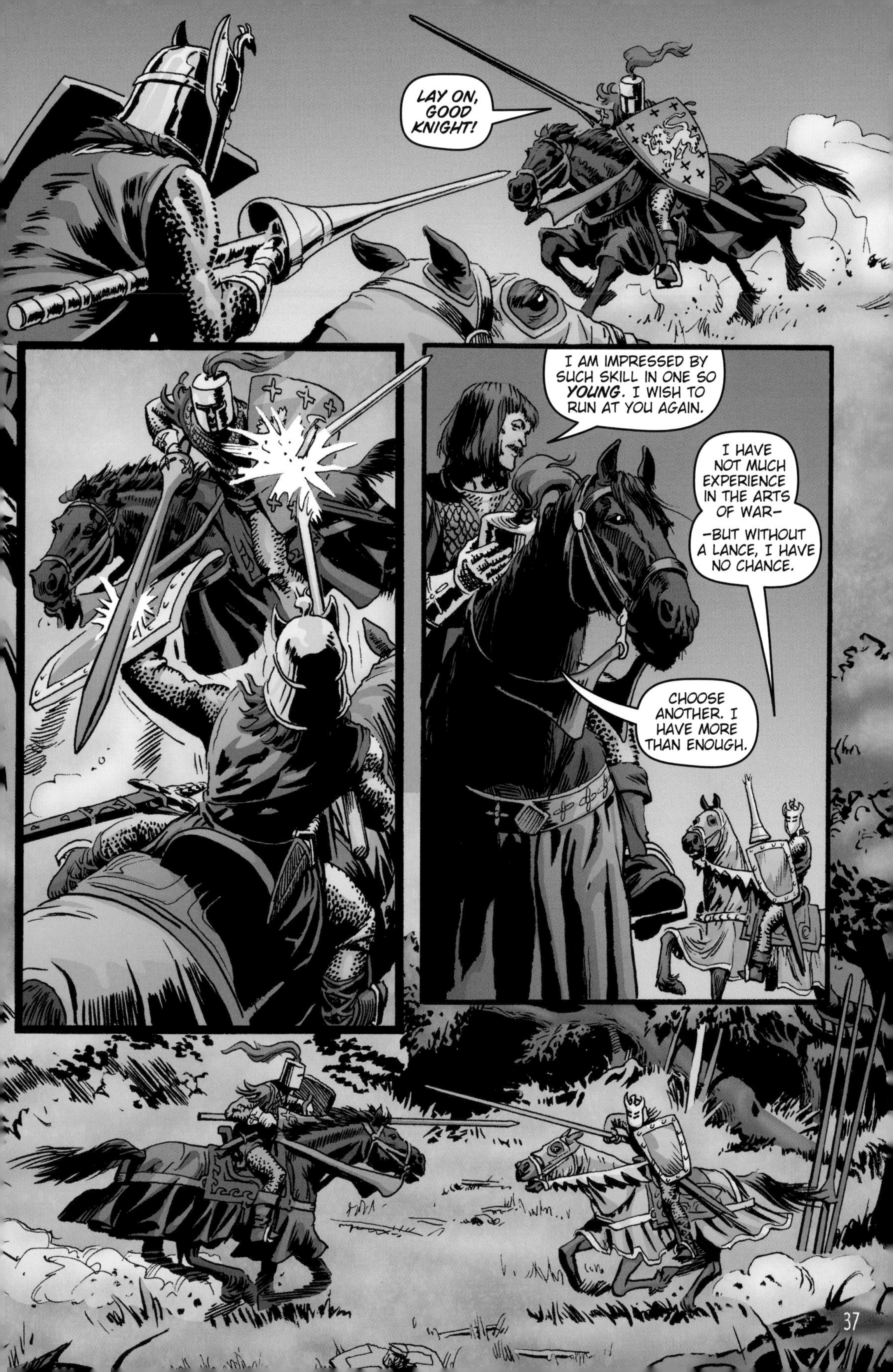
LAY ON, GOOD KNIGHT!
I AM IMPRESSED BY SUCH SKILL IN ONE SO *YOUNG*. I WISH TO RUN AT YOU AGAIN.
I HAVE NOT MUCH EXPERIENCE IN THE ARTS OF WAR–
–BUT WITHOUT A LANCE, I HAVE NO CHANCE.
CHOOSE ANOTHER. I HAVE MORE THAN ENOUGH.

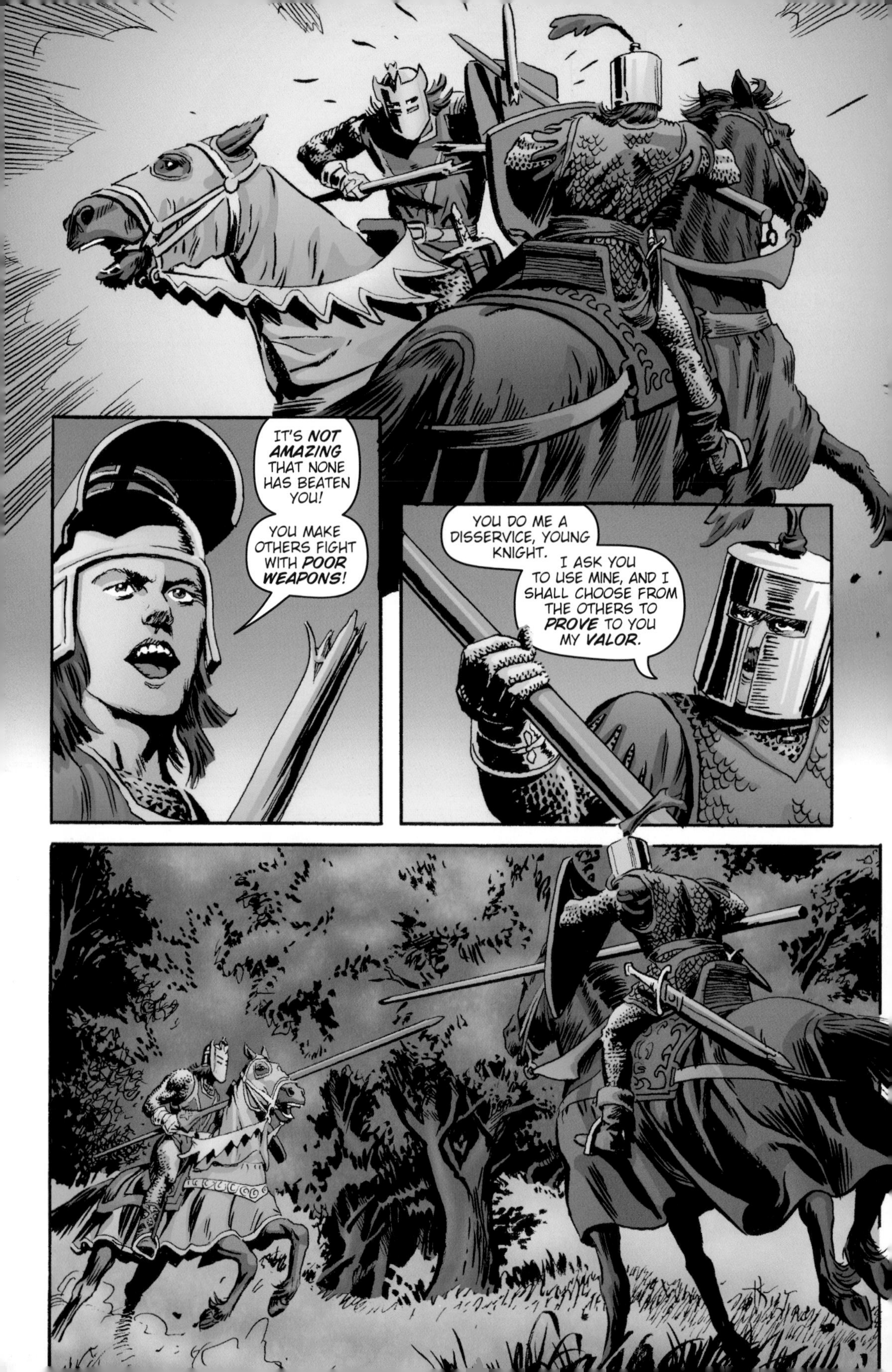
IT'S **NOT AMAZING** THAT NONE HAS BEATEN YOU!
YOU MAKE OTHERS FIGHT WITH **POOR WEAPONS**!
YOU DO ME A DISSERVICE, YOUNG KNIGHT.
I ASK YOU TO USE MINE, AND I SHALL CHOOSE FROM THE OTHERS TO **PROVE** TO YOU MY **VALOR**.

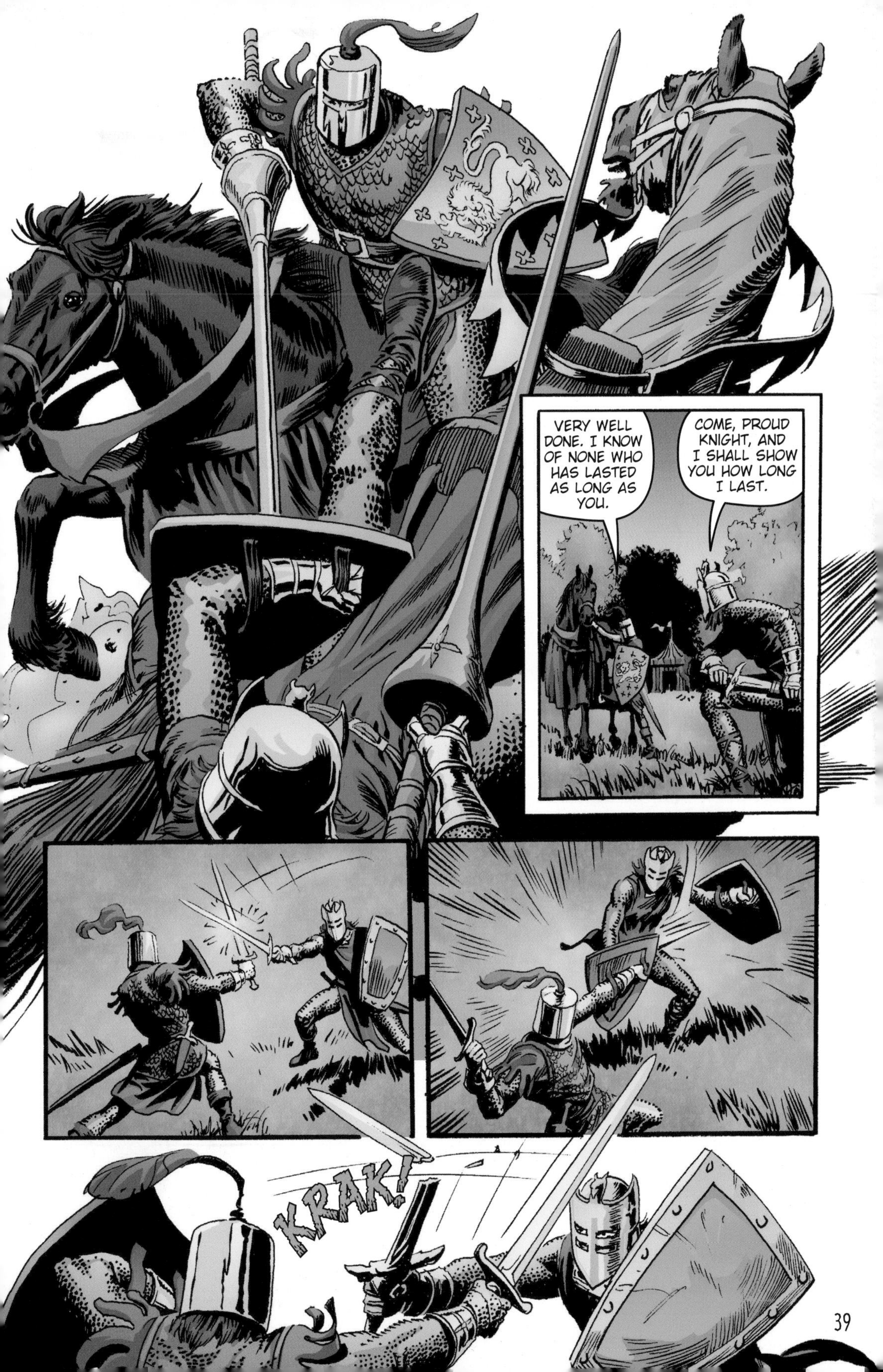
VERY WELL DONE. I KNOW OF NONE WHO HAS LASTED AS LONG AS YOU.
COME, PROUD KNIGHT, AND I SHALL SHOW YOU HOW LONG I LAST.
KRAK!

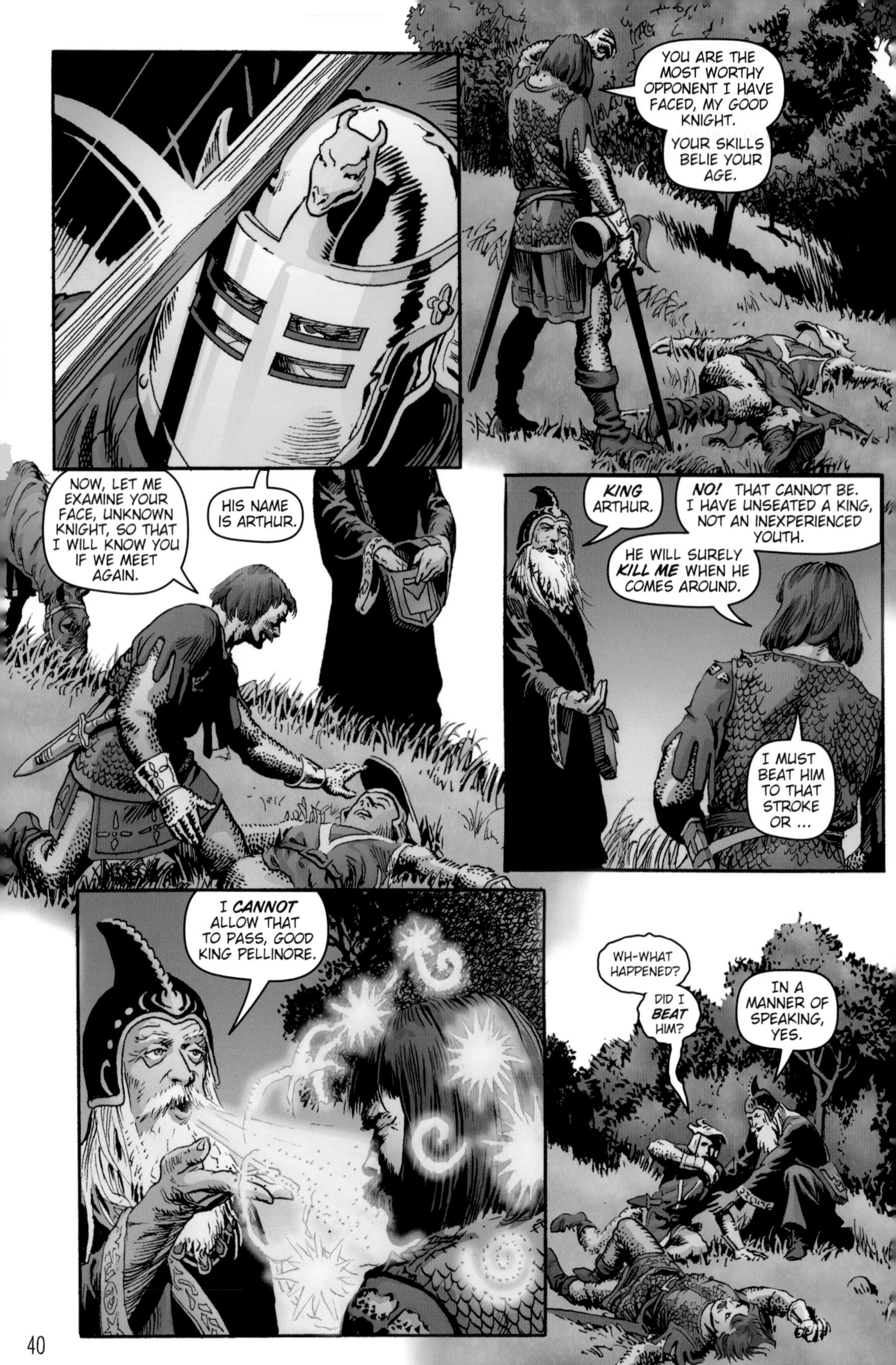
YOU ARE THE MOST WORTHY OPPONENT I HAVE FACED, MY GOOD KNIGHT.
YOUR SKILLS BELIE YOUR AGE.
NOW, LET ME EXAMINE YOUR FACE, UNKNOWN KNIGHT, SO THAT I WILL KNOW YOU IF WE MEET AGAIN.
HIS NAME IS ARTHUR.
KING ARTHUR.
NO! THAT CANNOT BE. I HAVE UNSEATED A KING, NOT AN INEXPERIENCED YOUTH.
HE WILL SURELY KILL ME WHEN HE COMES AROUND.
I MUST BEAT HIM TO THAT STROKE OR ...
I CANNOT ALLOW THAT TO PASS, GOOD KING PELLINORE.
WH-WHAT HAPPENED?
DID I BEAT HIM?
IN A MANNER OF SPEAKING, YES.

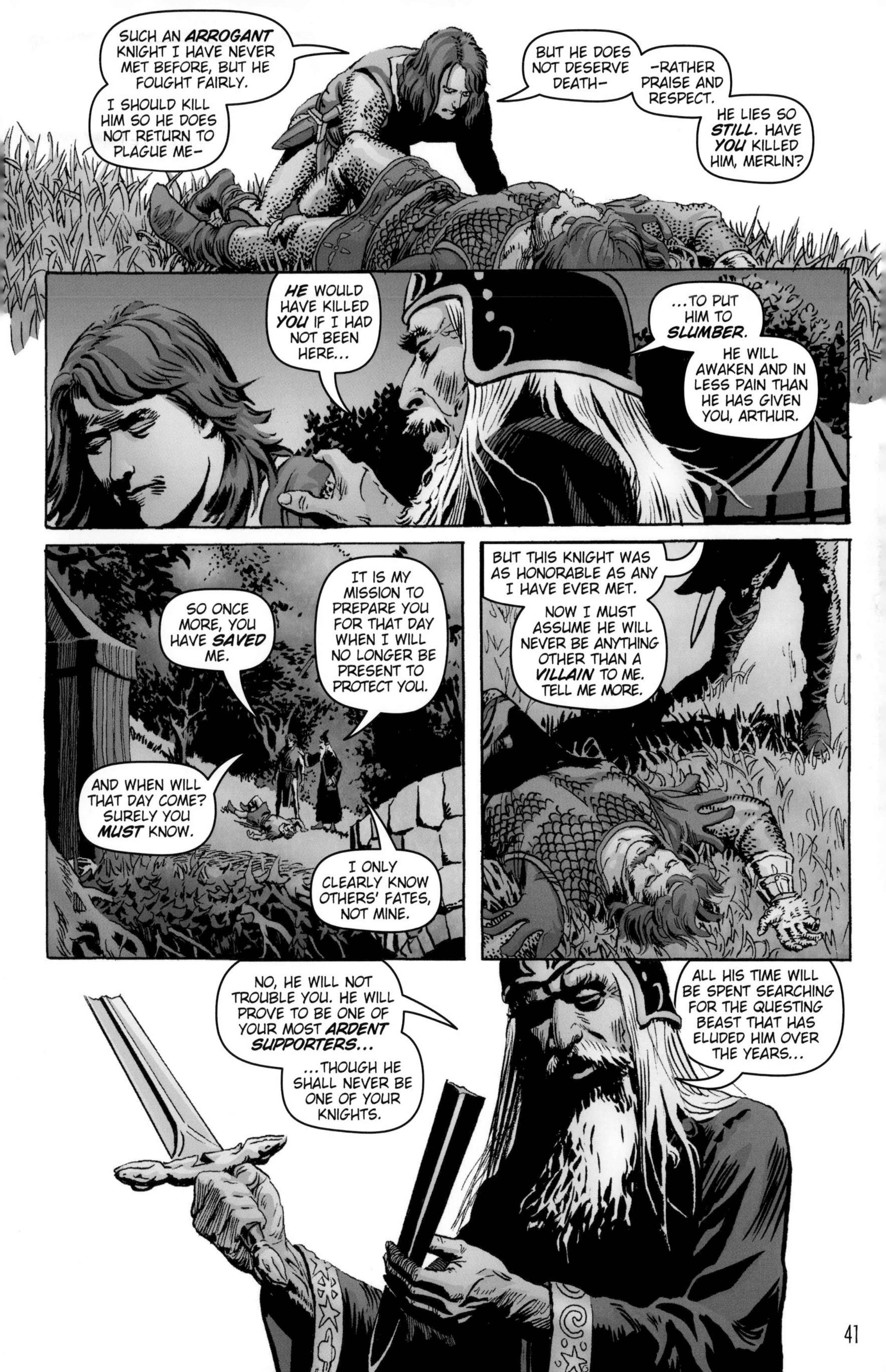

SUCH AN ARROGANT KNIGHT I HAVE NEVER MET BEFORE, BUT HE FOUGHT FAIRLY.
I SHOULD KILL HIM SO HE DOES NOT RETURN TO PLAGUE ME-
BUT HE DOES NOT DESERVE DEATH-
-RATHER PRAISE AND RESPECT.
HE LIES SO STILL. HAVE YOU KILLED HIM, MERLIN?
HE WOULD HAVE KILLED YOU IF I HAD NOT BEEN HERE...
...TO PUT HIM TO SLUMBER.
HE WILL AWAKEN AND IN LESS PAIN THAN HE HAS GIVEN YOU, ARTHUR.
SO ONCE MORE, YOU HAVE SAVED ME.
IT IS MY MISSION TO PREPARE YOU FOR THAT DAY WHEN I WILL NO LONGER BE PRESENT TO PROTECT YOU.
AND WHEN WILL THAT DAY COME? SURELY YOU MUST KNOW.
I ONLY CLEARLY KNOW OTHERS' FATES, NOT MINE.
BUT THIS KNIGHT WAS AS HONORABLE AS ANY I HAVE EVER MET.
NOW I MUST ASSUME HE WILL NEVER BE ANYTHING OTHER THAN A VILLAIN TO ME. TELL ME MORE.
NO, HE WILL NOT TROUBLE YOU. HE WILL PROVE TO BE ONE OF YOUR MOST ARDENT SUPPORTERS...
...THOUGH HE SHALL NEVER BE ONE OF YOUR KNIGHTS.
ALL HIS TIME WILL BE SPENT SEARCHING FOR THE QUESTING BEAST THAT HAS ELUDED HIM OVER THE YEARS...

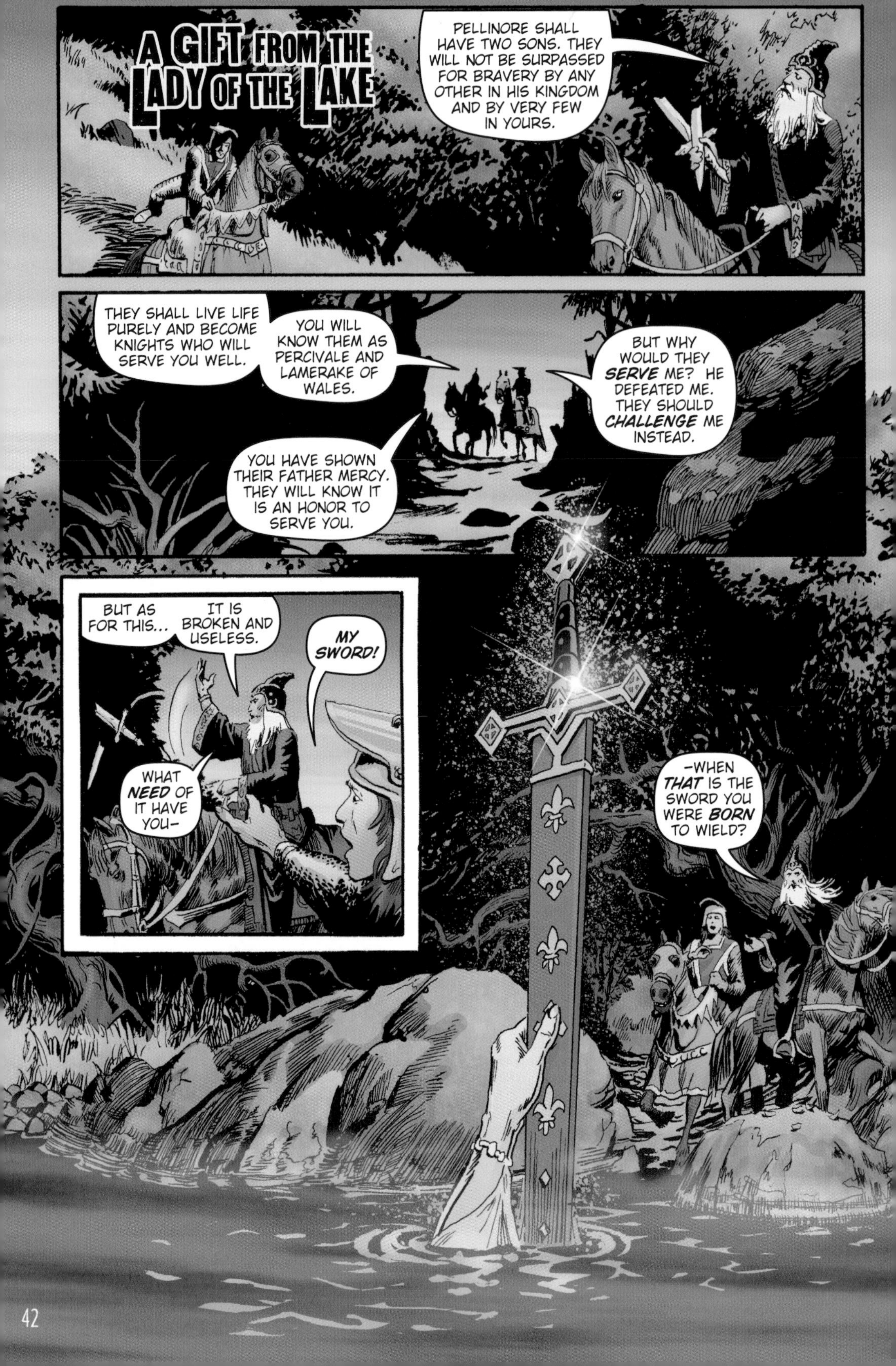
A GIFT FROM THE LADY OF THE LAKE
PELLINORE SHALL HAVE TWO SONS. THEY WILL NOT BE SURPASSED FOR BRAVERY BY ANY OTHER IN HIS KINGDOM AND BY VERY FEW IN YOURS.
THEY SHALL LIVE LIFE PURELY AND BECOME KNIGHTS WHO WILL SERVE YOU WELL.
YOU WILL KNOW THEM AS PERCIVALE AND LAMERAKE OF WALES.
BUT WHY WOULD THEY SERVE ME? HE DEFEATED ME. THEY SHOULD CHALLENGE ME INSTEAD.
YOU HAVE SHOWN THEIR FATHER MERCY. THEY WILL KNOW IT IS AN HONOR TO SERVE YOU.
BUT AS FOR THIS...
IT IS BROKEN AND USELESS.
MY SWORD!
WHAT NEED OF IT HAVE YOU-
-WHEN THAT IS THE SWORD YOU WERE BORN TO WIELD?

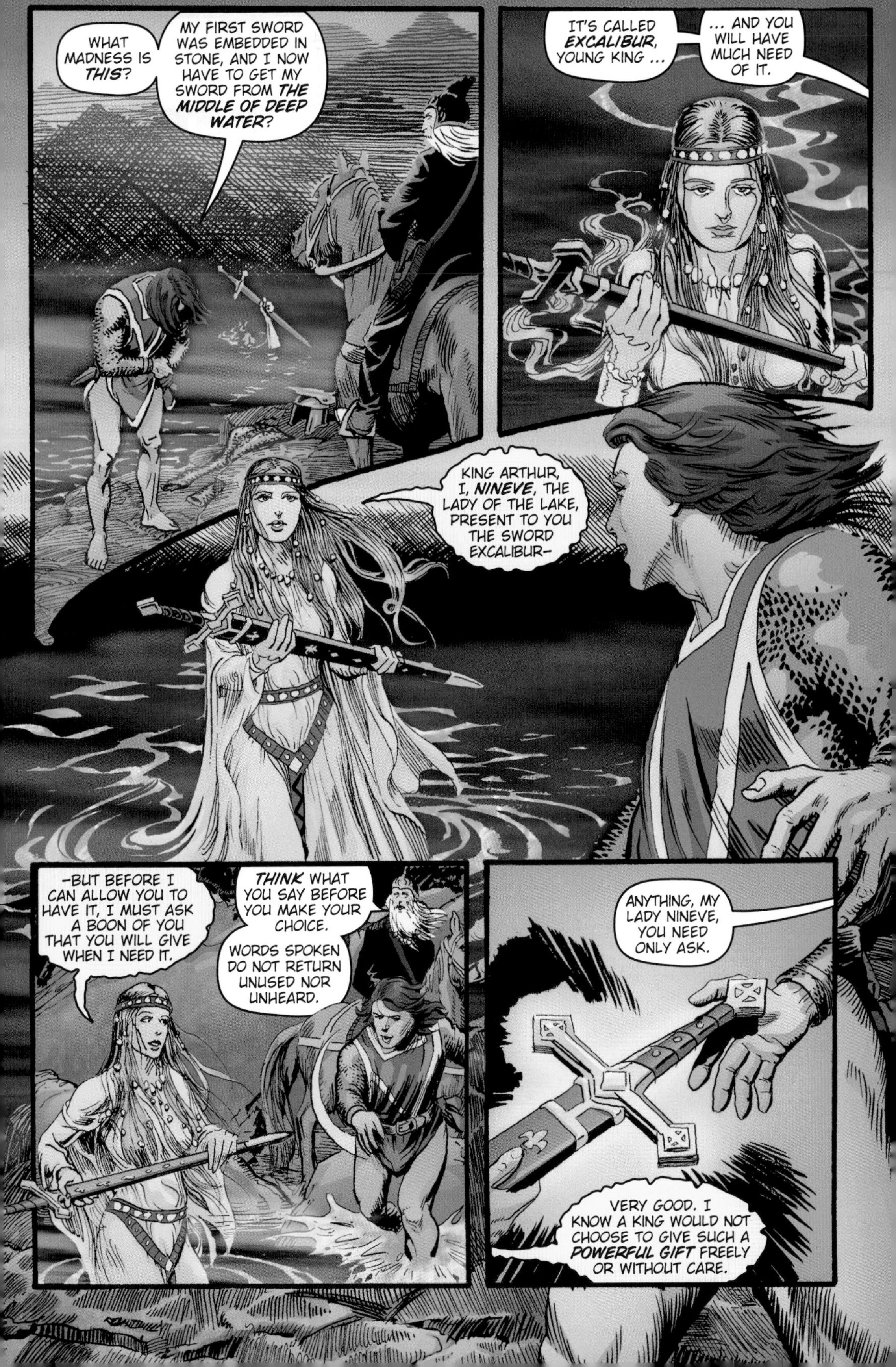
WHAT MADNESS IS THIS?
MY FIRST SWORD WAS EMBEDDED IN STONE, AND I NOW HAVE TO GET MY SWORD FROM THE MIDDLE OF DEEP WATER?
IT'S CALLED EXCALIBUR, YOUNG KING ...
... AND YOU WILL HAVE MUCH NEED OF IT.
KING ARTHUR, I, NINEVE, THE LADY OF THE LAKE, PRESENT TO YOU THE SWORD EXCALIBUR–
–BUT BEFORE I CAN ALLOW YOU TO HAVE IT, I MUST ASK A BOON OF YOU THAT YOU WILL GIVE WHEN I NEED IT.
THINK WHAT YOU SAY BEFORE YOU MAKE YOUR CHOICE.
WORDS SPOKEN DO NOT RETURN UNUSED NOR UNHEARD.
ANYTHING, MY LADY NINEVE, YOU NEED ONLY ASK.
VERY GOOD. I KNOW A KING WOULD NOT CHOOSE TO GIVE SUCH A POWERFUL GIFT FREELY OR WITHOUT CARE.

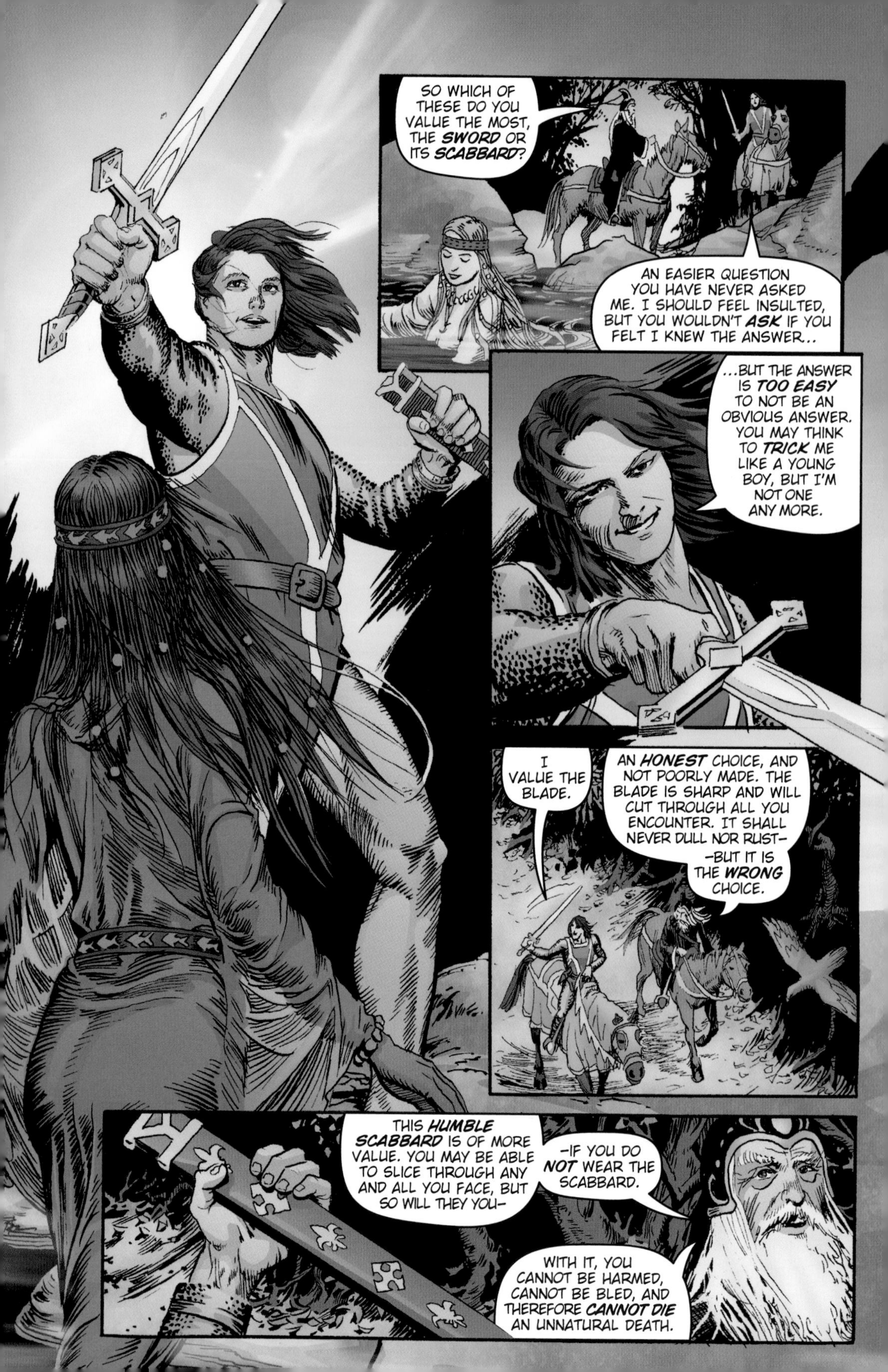
SO WHICH OF THESE DO YOU VALUE THE MOST, THE SWORD OR ITS SCABBARD?
AN EASIER QUESTION YOU HAVE NEVER ASKED ME. I SHOULD FEEL INSULTED, BUT YOU WOULDN'T ASK IF YOU FELT I KNEW THE ANSWER...
...BUT THE ANSWER IS TOO EASY TO NOT BE AN OBVIOUS ANSWER. YOU MAY THINK TO TRICK ME LIKE A YOUNG BOY, BUT I'M NOT ONE ANY MORE.
I VALUE THE BLADE.
AN HONEST CHOICE, AND NOT POORLY MADE. THE BLADE IS SHARP AND WILL CUT THROUGH ALL YOU ENCOUNTER. IT SHALL NEVER DULL NOR RUST–
–BUT IT IS THE WRONG CHOICE.
THIS HUMBLE SCABBARD IS OF MORE VALUE. YOU MAY BE ABLE TO SLICE THROUGH ANY AND ALL YOU FACE, BUT SO WILL THEY YOU–
–IF YOU DO NOT WEAR THE SCABBARD.
WITH IT, YOU CANNOT BE HARMED, CANNOT BE BLED, AND THEREFORE CANNOT DIE AN UNNATURAL DEATH.

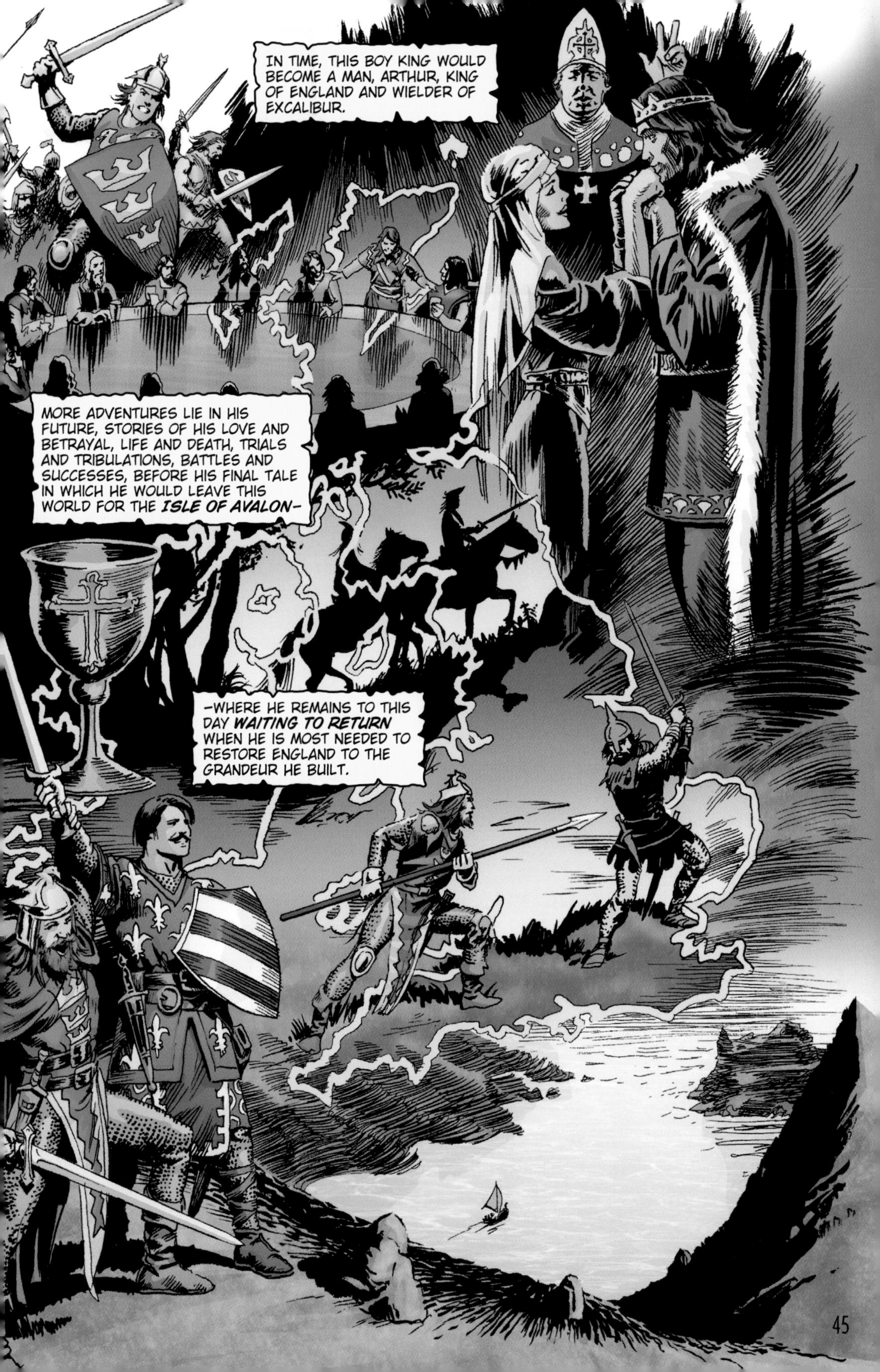
IN TIME, THIS BOY KING WOULD BECOME A MAN, ARTHUR, KING OF ENGLAND AND WIELDER OF EXCALIBUR.
MORE ADVENTURES LIE IN HIS FUTURE, STORIES OF HIS LOVE AND BETRAYAL, LIFE AND DEATH, TRIALS AND TRIBULATIONS, BATTLES AND SUCCESSES, BEFORE HIS FINAL TALE IN WHICH HE WOULD LEAVE THIS WORLD FOR THE ***ISLE OF AVALON***–
–WHERE HE REMAINS TO THIS DAY ***WAITING TO RETURN*** WHEN HE IS MOST NEEDED TO RESTORE ENGLAND TO THE GRANDEUR HE BUILT.

GLOSSARY

BOON: a favor given in answer to a request

CORONATION: a ceremony in which a ruler is crowned and takes possession of a kingdom. In England, traditionally, a king or queen is blessed by an archbishop, receives the royal robes, and has the crown placed on his or her head.

FACTION: a group within a larger group that fights against those in power. Factions may also fight against each other to gain power.

JOUST: a battle on horseback between two knights or among a group of knights. Jousts were often mock battles fought in tournaments. The purpose was to knock an opponent out of the saddle with a lance.

KNIGHT: a mounted soldier sworn to loyally serve a lord or ruler

LANCE: in jousting, a long, tapered spear carried by knights. In tournament jousts, lances had blunt tips and were made of dry wood. They broke easily without wounding or injuring contestants.

LIEGE: a superior, such as a lord or king, to whom others owe loyalty

LORD: a ruler or landowner with authority over a group of people

PAVILION: a small, temporary tent set up to hold a knight's weapons and armor during a tournament

PIKE: a short, heavy spear used by foot soldiers

SCABBARD: a sheath, or case, for a sword or knife

SENESCHAL: a person who manages the land and property of a lord

SQUIRE: a young person serving as a knight-in-training. Squires carried equipment, took care of horses, and performed other tasks for knights. In exchange, knights trained squires in combat and riding.

TOURNAMENT: a series of jousts or sporting battles fought at one time and place

WESTMINSTER: an area in south central England, part of modern-day London

WESTMINSTER ABBEY: a church and monastery, or religious house, at Westminster, England. The earliest monastery on the site dates back to the tenth century A.D. Westminster Abbey is the traditional site for all the coronations and burials of English kings and queens.

FURTHER READING AND WEBSITE

Crosley-Holland, Kevin. *The World of King Arthur and His Court: People, Places, Legend and Lore*. New York: Dutton Books, 2004. This illustrated guide provides information on key characters, daily life in a castle, knighthood, and other aspects of Arthurian legend.

King Arthur and the Knights of the Round Table
http://www.kingarthursknights.com
   This website provides articles on the historical and legendary Arthur, a map and information on Arthurian sites, artwork, and the stories of the knights and other characters of the famous legend.

Roberts, Jeremy. *King Arthur*. Minneapolis: Lerner Publications Company, 2001. This book examines both the historical and the literary Arthur, showing how he became a legendary hero.

Steinbeck, John. *The Acts of King Arthur and His Noble Knights*. 1952. Reprint, New York: Farrar, Straus and Giroux, 1993. Novelist John Steinbeck retells Malory's Le Morte d'Arthur as a collection of tales.

CREATING *EXCALIBUR UNSHEATHED*

In creating the story, author Jeff Limke adapted *Le Morte d'Arthur*, written about 1485 by Sir Thomas Malory, an English knight. Artist Thomas Yeates used historical and traditional sources to shape the story's visual details—from the heraldic colors to the buildings of medieval London. Together the text and the art paint a portrait of the "once and future king"—the man who saved Britain and, legend has it, will return again when his country most needs him.

original pencil sketch from page 8

INDEX

ABOUT THE AUTHOR AND THE ARTIST

JEFF LIMKE was raised in North Dakota, where he first read, listened to, and marveled at stories of Arthur and his knights. Limke later taught these stories for many years and has written several adaptations of them. Some of his stories have been published by Caliber Comics, Arrow Comics, and Kenzer and Company. Right now, it's very safe to assume he's reading even more stories about Arthurian legend.

THOMAS YEATES Originally from Sacramento, California, Thomas Yeates began his art training in high school and continued it at Utah State University and at Sacramento State. Subsequently, he was a member of the first class at Joe Kubert's School, a trade program for aspiring comic book artists in New Jersey. Yeates is strongly influenced in his craft by old-guard illustrators like Hal Foster, N. C. Wyeth, and Wallace Wood. He has worked as an illustrator for DC, Marvel, Dark Horse, and many other companies, drawing Tarzan, Zorro, the Swamp Thing, Timespirits, Captain America, and Conan, among others. He has also edited *Al Williamson: Hidden Lands* for Dark Horse.